DO NOT REMOVE
CARDS FROM POCKET

ALLEN COUNTY PUBLIC LIBRARY

FORT WAYNE, INDIANA 46802

You may return this book to any agency, branch,
or bookmobile of the Allen County Public Library.

DEMCO

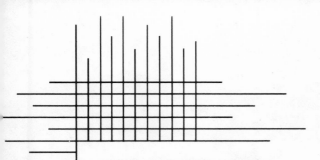

FORTRAN
for Beginners

FORTRAN
FOR
BEGINNERS

by Christopher Lampton

A GROLIER COMPANY

A Computer Literacy Skills Book

FRANKLIN WATTS   1984
New York   London   Toronto   Sydney

Library of Congress Cataloging in Publication Data

Lampton, Christopher.
    FORTRAN for beginners.

(A Computer literacy skills book)
Summary: An introduction to FORTRAN, the first major
computer language, including a language sampler and
step-by-step instructions for programming.
Includes index.
1. FORTRAN (Computer program language)—Juvenile
literature. [1. FORTRAN (Computer program language)
2. Programming languages (Computers)] I. Title.
II. Series.
QA76.73.F25L356   1984   001.64'24   83-26028
ISBN 0-531-04747-4

CONTENTS

2225930

1

FORTRAN— THE FIRST MAJOR COMPUTER LANGUAGE

Once upon a time, there were no such things as computers.

Actually, it wasn't all that long ago, though that may be hard to believe. Nowadays there seem to be computers wherever we look—on desktops, in microwave ovens, behind the dashboards of cars, on sale in drugstores. . . .

The modern computer goes back less than half a century, though the principles on which it is based are considerably older. The earliest computers were quite crude compared to the ones we have today.

A computer is nothing more or less than a machine for *processing* information. You put information into the computer in one form, and it comes back out in another, more useful form.

With the earliest computers, however, this information usually went into and came out of the computer in the form of numbers. Usually these numbers were zeros and ones. You might wonder what good it did anyone to feed a string of zeros and ones into a computer, just to get back another string of zeros and ones, in a somewhat different order.

As it happens, there is a special numbering system used by mathematicians called the *binary system,* which uses

Processing—Performing a series of operations on data and turning it into a new form.

Binary—A numbering system that uses only two digits—0 and 1.

only zeros and ones. You may have encountered the binary number system in your own math classes. The number 1 in binary is written as 1, just as in the decimal number system, which we ordinarily use. However, the number 2 is written as 10 and the number 3 as 11. Any number can be expressed in binary. The number 12, for instance, is 1100 in binary.

If you wanted to tell one of the early computers to add the numbers 2 and 7, for instance, you would need to translate the numbers 2 and 7 into their binary equivalents, which happen to be 10 and 111, respectively. The computer would then add the two numbers and respond with the binary number 1001, which is equivalent to 9.

First, however, it would also be necessary to tell the computer that you wanted it to add these two numbers, as opposed to subtracting them or multiplying them or whatever. In the earliest computers, this was done by actually going inside the computer and physically wiring it in such a way that it would perform addition. If you decided that you wanted to subtract the numbers instead, you would then have to reopen the computer and rewire it for subtraction rather than addition.

As you can imagine, this was an awkward system, and the physical rewiring of the computer was soon replaced by *programming*. With this system, the computer was wired only once, in such a way that it was capable of performing a multitude of different operations, such as subtraction, addition, etc. The computer was then given a series of instructions, called a *program,* that told it which of these operations it was expected to perform and in what order it was expected to perform them.

These programs were in the form of numbers—usually, once again, a string of zeros and ones. A program telling a computer to add two numbers together might have looked like this:

Program—A series of instructions to a computer written in a form that the computer is able to understand.

Programming—The creation of programs.

```
00111100
10011110
11110001
10101101
00011011
```

Since these numbers—or, rather, the instructions represented by them—constitute the language machines called
computers understand, we sometimes refer to them as
machine language. The above sequence of numbers, then,
is a machine-language program. Obviously, writing computer programs in machine language is a painstaking, exact-
ing task. Early on, many computer programmers began to
wonder if there might not be an easier way to write programs. As it turned out, there was: *high-level languages.*

With a high-level language you can write a sequence of
instructions to a computer—that is, a computer program—
as a series of English-sounding words. The computer itself
then translates those words into machine language, or a
string of zeros and ones. First, though, the computer must
have a program to tell it how to perform the translation.
This program, called a *compiler* or an *interpreter,* must
itself be written in machine language. Once a computer has

Machine language—The only computer language that
is directly executable by the central processing unit of a
computer.

High-level language—A symbolic computer language
that must be translated into machine language before it
can be executed by a computer.

Compiler—A computer program that translates high-
level language programs into machine-language programs.

Interpreter—A computer program that translates the
instructions in a high-level language program into
machine-language instructions while the program is
being executed.

been programmed to translate a high-level language into machine language, all further programming may be done in the high-level language.

It's not hard to write a computer program in a high-level language. You need only an understanding of what a computer is capable of doing and what the words are that will tell it to do that. Once your program is written, you give it to the computer (there are a number of ways for doing this) and the computer does the rest. Of course, learning to write programs for a computer and learning to write *good* programs for a computer are two different things, just as learning to speak the English language is not the same thing as learning to speak the English language well.

The first major high-level computer language was called FORTRAN. It was developed around 1957, by computer scientists working under the auspices of the IBM Corporation. The name FORTRAN is short for FORmula TRANslator. Originally, the language was intended for use by scientists and engineers and was particularly suitable for computing mathematical formulas, as its name implies. However, FORTRAN turned out to have a much broader appeal than that, and it is still popular with many programmers today. Furthermore, FORTRAN has had considerable influence over the development of newer computer languages, such as BASIC.

A quarter of a century ago, the use of FORTRAN was restricted to programmers working on large, expensive computers. Because these computers were large and expensive, they were used only for important tasks, and very few people ever had the privilege of writing programs for them. Today, almost anyone can have access to a computer, either at home or at school, and though most of the newer computers are much smaller, physically, than the giant computers of a quarter-century ago, many of them are just as powerful, if not more so, in terms of computing ability. Most of these small computers, which we term microcomputers, come with a built-in high-level language called BASIC. However, in many cases these computers can also be programmed in FORTRAN.

Theoretically, any small computer can be programmed in FORTRAN, but in practice this is not always the case. Remember: Before a computer can be programmed in FORTRAN, it must first be programmed to *understand*

FORTRAN, that is, to translate FORTRAN programs into machine language. The program that actually performs this translation is called a FORTRAN compiler. Before you can program a computer in FORTRAN, you must first obtain a FORTRAN compiler for that computer. All large computers and most major microcomputers have FORTRAN compilers available.

This book is intended for those readers who wish to know something about the FORTRAN language and how to use it to write computer programs. It is not necessary that you have access to a computer with a FORTRAN compiler in order to benefit from reading this book, but it would certainly help. If you do have a compiler, we will attempt to lead you step by step through the development of some simple FORTRAN programs. By the time you have finished, you should be ready to move on to more advanced instruction in the FORTRAN language.

If the lack of suitable equipment prevents you from following the examples in this book on an actual computer, you should nonetheless finish reading this book. By doing so, you will not only obtain a good overall knowledge of FORTRAN but also an understanding of what computer programming is all about.

* * * * * * * *

Before we consider how to program a computer, however, let's first consider the computer itself.

If a computer is a device for processing information, then it follows that there must be a way of getting information into the computer, and a way of getting it back out. And, in fact, there are many different devices, known collectively as *input/output devices,* I/O for short, that help you do both these things.

On a microcomputer, the most common input device is the *keyboard,* which works much like the keyboard on a

---

Input-output devices—Devices for moving data into a computer from the outside world and back out again.

Keyboard—A computer input device that allows the user to type input on a typewriterlike keyboard.

typewriter. When you type information on the keyboard of a microcomputer—usually in the form of words or numbers—that information is inputted directly to the computer.

The most common output device used by a microcomputer is the *video display*, which works much like the screen of an ordinary television. Information from inside the computer appears on the video display—once again, in the form of words or numbers—so that it can be read by the person using the computer.

When the FORTRAN language was originally developed, however, both keyboards and video displays were rarely used on computers. One reason for this is that keyboards and video displays are exceedingly slow methods of input/output, at least compared to the speeds at which computers are capable of working. It would be a waste of expensive computing time to force a computer to wait while a slow human being typed information on a keyboard, or read information from a video display. These same reasons don't apply on a microcomputer, since microcomputer time is quite cheap.

In the early days, the most common form of input/output was the *punch card*. In fact, punch cards are commonly used for input/output on large computers even today. A punch card, as its name implies, is little more than a strip of thin cardboard into which holes can be punched. These holes are punched with a machine called a *keypunch*, according to a special code that can be used to carry information. The machines that do the punching are controlled by a human keypunch operator and are very inexpensive to use. Once the holes have been punched, the punch cards can be presented to a computer, which then uses a device

Video display—A computer output device similar to a television set which displays data visually on a screen.

Punch card—A rectangular piece of cardboard on which information may be encoded as a series of punched holes and thus put into a computer.

called a *card reader* to read the information on the punch cards at high speeds. Thus, the information enters the computer with minimal expenditure of time. When the computer is ready to output information, it can print it out on high-speed printers, in a form that humans may then read at their leisure, while the computer proceeds to handle another task.

As we move on through this book, we will see how the use of punch cards has had a significant effect on the look of the FORTRAN language. However, it is unlikely, though not impossible, that you will be using punch cards on your own microcomputer, since card readers are usually either not available for microcomputers or are not really necessary for them.

In addition to devices for input and output of information, a computer system also requires methods of storing information, both temporarily and permanently. Every computer can store limited amounts of information temporarily in its memory, using a series of electronic circuits inside the computer itself. Information is stored in the computer's memory as a string of binary numbers. In fact, any kind of information that you put into a computer—numbers, words, even pictures—is immediately translated into binary numbers and stored in that form. The computer's memory is used to store both computer programs and the information, or *data,* that those programs process.

However, there is a limit to how much information a computer's memory can store. Memory can fill up very quickly. Furthermore, when the computer is turned off, the information in its internal memory vanishes, as though it had never existed. Therefore, a more permanent form of information storage is also required by the computer, a form of storage that can be used to hold information that

---

Card reader—A computer peripheral device for reading punch cards and moving the information encoded on the cards into the computer.

Data—Information to be processed, or that has been processed, by a computer program.

the computer's internal memory has no room for at the moment, or to hold information after the computer has been turned off.

There are two common forms of mass information storage: tape and disk. In both cases, the information is stored in the form of magnetic impulses on a specially treated surface. In the first case, this surface is in the form of magnetic tape, either on a reel or a cassette, though most microcomputers use tape cassettes rather than reels. In the latter case, the surface is that of a magnetic disk. In most microcomputer systems, these so-called *floppy disks* look rather like thin plastic phonograph records inside protective paper jackets. Because these devices—tape and disk—can store large amounts of information, they are collectively known as *mass storage devices*. Other mass storage devices are currently being developed, but these two are the most common at the moment.

If you are planning to try on a microcomputer the examples in this book, the computer must have at minimum a keyboard, or equivalent input device; a video display, or perhaps a printer; a disk drive; and at least 48K of internal memory storage. (K is a measure of a computer's memory. It is short for kilobyte, or 1,024 bytes. A *byte* is the amount of memory required to store a single character, such as a letter of the alphabet, or a punctuation mark, or—in many instances—a single machine-language instruction. Therefore, a computer with 48K of internal memory is capable of storing up to 48,000 characters.)

Before the computer can be programmed in FORTRAN, you must also have a FORTRAN system available. The FORTRAN system consists of several programs,

---

Mass-storage device—Peripheral device used to store information more or less permanently away from the main computer memory.

Floppy disk—A mass-storage device used for storing computer data in magnetic form on a disk.

Byte—A unit of data made up of eight binary digits (bits).

including the FORTRAN compiler, to translate FOR-
TRAN programs into machine language, plus a FOR-
TRAN editor, a special program that helps you to type
FORTRAN programs and save them on magnetic disk.
Some FORTRAN systems will also include a program
called a *linker,* or *loader,* which finishes the translation process begun by the compiler. Lastly, but by no means least
importantly, the FORTRAN system should also include a
manual, which will explain the workings of these various
programs. The manual will offer specific instructions on
how to type FORTRAN programs, as well as instructions
on how to operate the compiler that translates these programs into machine language. You would do well to read
through the manual before you begin using the system, con-
centrating especially on those portions that tell you how to
use the editor and how to run the compiler and the linker.

The programs in the FORTRAN system—that is, the
editor, the linker, and the compiler—will almost certainly
be on a magnetic disk. At some point you will need to insert
this disk into the disk drive, the device attached to the computer that reads the information stored on the surface of the
disk. When we ask the computer to take a program stored
on a disk and move it into the computer's internal memory, where the computer will be able to follow the instructions in the program, we say that we are "loading the program." The manual will tell you how to load the editor, the
compiler, and the linker. Later, when we write programs of
our own, it will be possible for us to move them out of the
computer's memory and onto the disk for storage. This is
called "saving a program to disk." The manual should also
give instructions for doing this.

Incidentally, though the FORTRAN language was
developed in 1957, it has changed somewhat over the years.
In 1966, a standard version of the language was arrived at
by the American National Standards Institute (ANSI). This
version of FORTRAN is called FORTRAN IV and is the

Linker—A program that links a compiled FORTRAN
program together with subroutines necessary for the
program's proper execution.

version generally available for microcomputers; thus, it is the version we will consider in this book. For instance, there is a version of FORTRAN IV available for the Apple called Apple FORTRAN and a version for the TRS-80 called Microsoft FORTRAN, also available as Radio Shack FORTRAN. Microsoft FORTRAN is also available for CP/M systems. In 1978, an improved FORTRAN standard was developed: FORTRAN 77. But at this writing, there are few, if any, FORTRAN 77 compilers available for microcomputers. In the unlikely event that you have a FORTRAN 77 compiler, however, all the programs in this book should still run on it, although in some cases there may be easier ways to write these programs in FORTRAN 77 than in FORTRAN IV. Still, the principles of FORTRAN programming will be the same, whether you are using FORTRAN IV or FORTRAN 77.

Assuming that you have now looked at your FORTRAN manual—that is, if you are following along with a computer—we are now ready to plunge headfirst into FORTRAN programming, with a look at our first FORTRAN program!

Suggested Projects

Examine your computer and see if you can identify which parts of the system are used for input, which for output, and which for external memory storage. (Some parts may be used for more than one of these functions.) Read the computer manual for any special rules pertaining to the use of these devices.

2

A FORTRAN SAMPLER

A program is simply a series of instructions telling a computer what we wish it to do. In general, the computer will perform these instructions in the order in which they are given, though there are a number of ways in which we can deliberately cause the computer to take the instructions out of order, if we so desire.

Let's start out by examining a complete FORTRAN program for performing a simple task: computing the average of nine test grades. Do not expect to understand this program completely, or to be able to write a program like it—not right away, at least. We'll cover all this material again later, in much more detail. Consider this program as an example, to give you an overall idea of what FORTRAN programming is about before we get down to particulars.

Here's the program:

```
00100                   PROGRAM AVERAGE
00200      C    COMPUTE THE AVERAGE OF NINE
                       GRADES
00300           TOTAL = 0
00400           DO   10 I=1,9
00500             READ(5,11)GRADE
00600      11    FORMAT(F3.1)
00700             TOTAL = TOTAL + GRADE
00800      10    CONTINUE
00900           AVERAG = TOTAL/10
01000           WRITE(5,21)AVERAG
01100      21    FORMAT('0THE AVERAGE IS   ',F3.1)
01200           IF (AVERAG .GT. 80)WRITE (5,31)
01300      31    FORMAT('THAT''S A GOOD AVERAGE')
```

```
01400              IF (AVERAG .LT. 80)WRITE(5,41)
01500      41      FORMAT('THAT''S A PRETTY LOUSY
01600              – AVERAGE')
01700              IF (AVERAG .EQ. 80)WRITE(5,51)
01800      51      FORMAT('THAT''S NOT BAD')
01900              STOP
02000              END
```

Let's examine this program line by line. Once again, do not expect to understand everything that's going on here, but do refer back to appropriate parts of the program as we explain it. We'll be coming back to this material in later chapters, and you might want to refer back to this section again at that time.

Notice first of all that the program is laid out in a distinct pattern, as though the page of the book were broken into imaginary columns. This is, in fact, the case. The first column, on the far left-hand side of the page, is made up entirely of line numbers. These numbers are not actually part of the program and are put there by the FORTRAN editor to make the program easier to type, and to change, after you've finished typing it. Some versions of FORTRAN may not include these line numbers, and we will not often show them in future programs. You will not have to type these numbers yourself; in fact, your FORTRAN editor probably will not allow you to type these numbers yourself. When you type a line of a FORTRAN program, you will most likely begin typing a few spaces to the right of these numbers.

The second column, immediately to the right of the line numbers, is largely blank. Only certain kinds of information go into this area. The letter C on the second line, for instance, tells us that the remainder of that line is a *comment*—a statement placed in the program for the programmer's own reference, but completely ignored by the compiler when it translates the program into machine language. The C must be placed in the very first typing position.

Comment—A remark embedded within a FORTRAN program, ignored by the computer but retained for the sake of human readers.

You'll also notice a series of numbers in this column. These numbers are sometimes called *labels*. They identify certain lines of the program, so that those lines can be referred to in other lines of the program, as we shall see.

The next major area begins with the eighth typing position. This area contains the actual program instructions. These instructions are divided into two types: *executable instructions* and *nonexecutable instructions.*

An executable instruction will actually be translated into machine language by the compiler. A nonexecutable instruction, on the other hand, will not be translated into machine language. Rather, it is a note to the compiler, giving the compiler information it will need concerning the translation of the rest of the program. Executable and nonexecutable instructions will be mixed together throughout the program, though certain nonexecutable instructions must always go at the beginning of a program.

The first line of our program begins with the word PRO-GRAM. This is a nonexecutable instruction that serves to give the program a name—in this case, AVERAGE—by which it can be referred to at a later time. Not all FOR-TRAN compilers will recognize the PROGRAM instruction. It is not part of the FORTRAN IV standard, though it is nonetheless included in many compilers. (All FORTRAN 77 compilers should recognize it.) For this reason, however, we will not include it in future programs, although the word PROGRAM may appear in comments.

The next line is the comment we mentioned earlier. As a comment, it is not executable and is therefore completely ignored by the compiler. It simply serves to tell us what the

---

Label—A number given to a line of a FORTRAN program for reference elsewhere in the program.

Executable instruction—A FORTRAN instruction that is translated directly into machine language by the compiler.

Nonexecutable instruction—A FORTRAN instruction representing a message to the compiler, telling it how to compile the rest of the program.

program does, should we come back to it at a later date and not be able to recall. It also helps make the program more readable to other programmers who may come in contact with it. It is always good to make a program as readable as possible. This facilitates our making later changes in the program, should they become necessary.

The next line reads TOTAL = 0. This requires some explanation. The word TOTAL is a *variable*, which is a kind of identifier, representing a location in the computer's memory. This location is large enough to hold a number of considerable size. In this instruction, however, we are simply telling the machine to store the number 0 in that location. We will see why in a moment.

The next instruction, DO 10 I=1,9 (called a DO loop), is a very complex one, and we will simply touch on it here, rather than try to explain exactly how it works. Later, we will analyze it in some detail, when we come to the chapter on program loops. Simply put, it tells the computer to repeat a series of instructions nine times. Which instructions is the computer to repeat? All instructions between the word DO and the line labeled 10. When a computer repeats a series of instructions, we refer to this series of instructions as a program *loop*. Loops are extremely important in computer programming. (Note: throughout this book, the symbol I is an uppercase letter i, not the numeral 1.)

The word READ in the next line is FORTRAN's all-purpose input statement. It is an executable statement that tells the computer to accept information from an input device. The specifics of this input are contained in parentheses after the word READ, like this: READ(5,11). The first number in parentheses, 5, tells us which input device the information is to come from. On the FORTRAN system used by the author of this book (Microsoft FORTRAN), input device number 5 is the computer's keyboard. Thus,

---

Variable—A name, or label, given to the portion of the computer's memory where data will be stored.

Loop—A set of instructions in a program that will be executed more than once in a single program run.

when this statement is executed, the computer will pause and wait for the user to type information on the keyboard. This information will then be stored in a location in the computer's memory labeled GRADE.

Notice that this program has several statements in it beginning with the word FORMAT. These are called, appropriately enough, FORMAT statements. They are nonexecutable, but they contain important information concerning the way in which the computer should perform the input requested by the READ statement. The second number in parentheses after the word READ, 11, refers to a FORMAT statement elsewhere in the program. Which FORMAT statement does it refer to? Why, the one labeled 11—which just happens to be in the next line, though it could have been placed anywhere in the program. The FORMAT statement itself reads FORMAT(F3.1). The number in parentheses is called a *field descriptor,* and it tells the computer just what sort of input to expect. In loose terms, this particular field descriptor tells the computer to expect a number. (Actually, it tells it a great deal more than that, as we shall see in Chapter Five.) At this point, the person using the computer is expected to type the first in the series of ten grades to be averaged. The value typed will be stored in the computer's memory at the location identified by variable GRADE.

Remember the location in the computer's memory we created with the name TOTAL? The next line makes another reference to it. This line adds the value stored at the location called GRADE—which was inputted from the keyboard by the user, as we saw in the last paragraph—to the current value stored at the location called TOTAL, which is a 0. It then stores the result back in location TOTAL.

Finally, the next line simply reads CONTINUE. The word CONTINUE does nothing, though it has a purpose for existing, which we shall see later. This line is labeled 10, which means that it is the end of the loop we started four lines earlier. The sequence of instructions that we have just

---

Field descriptor—A symbolic description of the format in which data is to be input or output by the computer.

traced will be repeated nine more times, which means that the user will type in nine more grades, one each time the READ statement is repeated. Furthermore, each new value stored at location GRADE will be added to the value stored at location TOTAL, which means that TOTAL will eventually contain the total of all ten grades.

After this section finishes looping ten times, the computer computes the average of the ten grades, by dividing the value stored at TOTAL by the number of grades. This is done by the statement AVERAG = TOTAL/10. This is the standard method of computing an average; you've probably used it yourself. The result of this division is stored at a new location called AVERAG. (A better name for this location might be AVERAGE, but most versions of FORTRAN allow only six characters in a variable name.)

The WRITE statement, in the next line, is FORTRAN's all-purpose output statement. It works much like the READ statement, except that it outputs information to a chosen device instead of inputting it. In this case, it is outputting to device number 5, which on the author's FORTRAN system is the video display. It performs this output according to the instructions in the FORMAT statement labeled 21. This FORMAT statement looks rather like the last one, except that it also contains a message in quotation marks. This tells the computer to write the message on the video display exactly as it is written in the FORMAT statement: "THE AVERAGE IS ". Well, not *exactly* as it's written in the FORMAT statement; you'll notice that there is a 0 at the beginning of the program sentence that does not appear in the displayed version. That's because this zero also has a special meaning, as we will see. Following the sentence, the computer writes the value stored at location AVERAG. If that value is 73.6, say, the computer will write THE AVERAGE IS 73.6 on the video display.

The program climaxes with a series of conditional statements. These are executable statements that allow the computer to make decisions based on the information that it has processed. Each of these statements begins with the word IF. Upon encountering this word, the computer then begins to evaluate the information contained in parentheses after the IF. If this information is true, then the computer performs the action following the parentheses. If the information is false, the computer does not perform the action following the parentheses. What could be simpler?

In this case, all of the conditional statements involve the value stored at AVERAG. The first such statement, for instance, reads IF (AVERAG .GT. 80) WRITE (5,31). .GT. in FORTRAN means "greater than." In other words, if the value stored at location AVERAG is greater than 80, then the computer should write to the video screen the sentence given in FORMAT statement 31, which reads 'THAT''S A GOOD AVERAGE'. Notice how the apostrophe in the word THAT''S has been doubled to distinguish it from the single quote marks around the sentence.

Similarly, the next IF statement tells the computer to write the sentence 'THAT''S A PRETTY LOUSY AVERAGE' if the value stored at AVERAG is less than (.LT.) 80. And the final IF statement tells the computer to write the sentence 'THAT''S NOT BAD' if the value stored at AVERAG happens to be equal to (.EQ.) 80.

One other thing you might want to notice. The statement in line 1500 spills over the end of the line and is continued on line 1600. FORTRAN allows us to do this, but we must tell the compiler that we are doing it. By putting a character—any character—in the seventh column, right before the statement section begins, we indicate that the line that follows is a continuation of the previous line. In this manner, we can continue program statements for as many lines as we wish.

And that's the program, except for the words STOP and END. At first acquaintance, these two instructions might seem to mean the same thing. In fact, they mean two different things altogether. The word STOP is an executable statement. It tells the computer to stop executing the program and return to its normal state. This will take place while the program is actually being run on the computer (in the computer's own language, machine language, of course). The word END, on the other hand, is a nonexecutable statement. It is obeyed by the compiler while the original FORTRAN program is being compiled (translated) into machine language. END tells the compiler that the program is over and that the compilation process may now cease.

This program doesn't really do much. It just takes ten

numbers from the keyboard of the computer, adds them together, computes and prints an average, and makes an appropriate comment. But it does illustrate a great many of the principles that we will be studying in detail in upcoming chapters: program loops, conditional statements, input/ output, storage of values in memory, etc. And by the end of this book you will probably be able to write FORTRAN programs at least as complex as this and perhaps a great deal more so.

Suggested Projects

Look at the manual for your FORTRAN system and see if it contains a reference section listing the various instructions that the compiler understands. Compare this list to the instructions in the example program above. If there are brief descriptions of each command in the list, read these descriptions and see if you can understand how they relate to our use of similar commands in the example. There is no need to fully understand how each command works, but see if you can grasp the gist of each one.

VARIABLES
AND NUMBERS

During the execution of a computer program, it is usually necessary for the computer to store certain amounts of information. In FORTRAN, as in most computer languages, this storage is accomplished through the use of variables.

What is a variable? It is a name that represents a storage location in the computer's memory. The name must begin with a letter of the alphabet. That letter, in turn, can be followed by numbers or more letters, up to a total length of six characters. Characters other than letters or numbers, such as punctuation marks, are not valid. The following are valid FORTRAN variable names:

TOTAL
NUMBER
H12345
I
G3W8

Here are some invalid names for FORTRAN variables:

1WAY
HI-FI
PROBLEM
654321
HELLO?

Can you see why each of these variable names is unacceptable?

We store a value at a location in the computer's memory with an *assignment statement*. An assignment statement consists of the name of a variable followed by an equals sign ("=") and the value that we wish to store at that location. A typical FORTRAN assignment statement looks like this:

COST = 14.95

This stores the value 14.95 in the location in the computer's memory that we have termed COST. This is called "assigning a value to a variable," or "setting a variable equal to a value." The following is also a valid FORTRAN assignment statement:

RESULT = 2 + 4

This is a bit fancier than the last. We have now required the computer to perform a little arithmetic before it can store a value at the location we have called RESULT. First, the computer must add the numbers 2 and 4 together, then store their sum—the number 6—at location RESULT.

Incidentally, there is a special term we use to describe a sequence of values and arithmetic operations such as 2 + 4. We call it an *arithmetic expression*. An arithmetic expression is a series of arithmetic operations, performed on numbers and variables, that can be reduced to a single value. The arithmetic expression 4 + 2 − 1, for instance, can be reduced to the value 5. We will see arithmetic expressions (and other kinds of expressions) popping up quite often in FORTRAN. The following are examples of arithmetic expressions:

7 + 10 / 14
8 * VALUE
THIS**4

Assignment statement—An instruction that assigns a value to a variable.

Arithmetic expression—A series of numbers, variables, and arithmetic operators that can be reduced to a single numeric value.

```
NUMBER + OTHER
1176
RESULT
```

Some of these mathematical symbols may be unfamiliar to you at the moment, but they will be explained later in this chapter. For now it is important that you realize that both variables and numbers are allowed in expressions, and that a single number or variable can be considered a complete expression by itself. The primary qualification for an arithmetic expression is that it be equal to a single numerical value. Expressions will appear in a number of different places in FORTRAN statements, not just on the right side of an assignment statement.

Once we've assigned a value to a variable, the computer will treat that variable as though it actually were that value. For instance, the following series of FORTRAN instructions actually performs the same job as the last assignment statement we showed you, but in a slightly more complex manner:

```
FIRST = 2
SECOND = 4
RESULT = FIRST + SECOND
```

The first line assigns a value of 2 to variable FIRST, and the second line assigns a value of 4 to variable SECOND. Then the third line adds the values stored at these two locations and assigns the result—the number 6—to location RESULT.

In our description so far, we have greatly oversimplified one aspect of FORTRAN programming—the way that FORTRAN handles numbers. Actually, there are several different kinds of numbers dealt with by FORTRAN, and the programmer must be aware of the differences between them. The two most common kinds of numbers are *integers* and *real numbers.*

Integer—A number that may not have a fractional (decimal) value.

Real number—A number that may have a fractional (decimal) value.

An integer, sometimes referred to as a "whole number," is the kind of number you count with: 1, 2, 3 4, 5, 6, etc. An integer cannot have a fractional value. For instance, the number 4.5 is not an integer. On most computers an integer must fall within a certain range of values. On microcomputers, this range is generally from −32768 to 32768. A number that falls outside this range is not an integer, even if it has no fractional value.

A real number, on the other hand, can have a fractional value and can be of any size you wish—theoretically, anyway. In practice, real numbers above a certain size—about a million, on most computers—must be written in floating point notation, a system that we will not be discussing here. If you wish to know more about floating point numbers, you should consult an advanced programming text.

We must always tell the computer whether we wish it to store a number in its memory as an integer or as a real number. This affects the amount of memory storage the computer allots for the number. On microcomputers, FORTRAN generally allots two bytes of memory storage for integers and four bytes for real numbers. The choice also affects the kind of arithmetic the computer performs on the numbers. Arithmetic performed on integer numbers is much faster and more efficient than arithmetic performed on real numbers, for instance. For this reason, we should really use integers wherever we have no need for fractional values or very large numbers.

How do we tell the computer what kinds of numbers we want to use? There are many ways. When we write a number in a program with a fractional value, for instance, the computer knows automatically that the number is a real number. Even if it doesn't have a fractional value, if we write a number followed by a decimal point and a zero, such as 76.0, the computer will automatically assume it to be real. On the other hand, a number without a fractional value will be assumed to be an integer.

Note, however, that we must also use different kinds of variables to store these different types of numbers. *Integer variables* are used to store integer numbers and *real vari-*

Integer variable—A variable that may be assigned an integer value.

ables are used to store real numbers. Once again, we must tell the FORTRAN compiler what type of variable we are using, and there are a number of different ways of doing this.

For instance, unless we tell it otherwise, the FORTRAN compiler assumes that all variables starting with the letters I through N are integer variables. (This is easy enough to remember, since I and N are the first two letters of the word "integer.") All other variables are assumed to be real variables. These are called *default variables,* since all variables beginning with a certain letter will become a certain kind of variable by default. The following are legitimate FORTRAN integer variables:

I
INDEX
NUMBER
ITOTAL
J1111
MOTHER

However, should we decide that we would like some integer variables that do not begin with the letters I through N, we can declare them explicitly. We do this by writing the word INTEGER followed by the names of the integer variables we wish to use, like this:

INTEGER TOTAL, EGGS

This declares that the variables TOTAL and EGGS are integer variables. INTEGER is a nonexecutable FORTRAN statement. That is, it is simply a message to the compiler, telling it that these variables will from now on be used to store integer numbers. Such a statement must come close to the beginning of the program, before any executable statements and certainly before the variables are actually used in the program.

We can similarly declare variables to be real variables, with the word REAL, like this:

Real variable—A variable that may be assigned a real value.

REAL NUMBER, IGLOO, JUPITER

This declares the variables NUMBER, IGLOO, and JUPITER to be real variables.

Finally, if we simply decide that we don't like the way FORTRAN decides which variables are integer and which are real, we can change the whole system, with an IMPLICIT statement. The IMPLICIT statement declares that variables beginning with certain letters of the alphabet are automatically either real or integer, like this:

IMPLICIT REAL (I-K)

This declares that all variables beginning with the letters I through K are to be considered real variables, even though normally they are considered integer. We can also do the same thing with integer variables, if we desire.

Generally, we will use IMPLICIT statements only when we wish to change all variables in a program to a certain type, like this:

IMPLICIT INTEGER (A-Z)

This declares that all variables beginning with the letters A through Z—which is to say, all variables—are to be considered integer variables. Of course, we can override this by explicitly declaring certain variables to be real. An IMPLICIT statement must come at the very beginning of a program, before any explicit declarations have been made.

There are other types of numbers—and variables—in FORTRAN as well, though you will use them less often. A *byte number* is a number that can be stored in a single byte of memory. It must fall within the range of 0 to 255 and cannot be negative or have a fractional value. Byte numbers are used for a few specialized applications, such as storing letters of the alphabet. (Computers generally store letters as numbers.)

There are no default byte variables, however; they must be declared explicitly, using the word BYTE, like this:

Byte number—A variable that may be assigned a single byte (eight-bit) value.

BYTE NUMBER, VALUE, LETTER

This declares the variables NUMBER, VALUE, and LETTER to be byte variables. FORTRAN also offers *double-precision variables*. These are a special kind of real variable that use extra memory space, usually eight bytes, for storing a value. The accuracy of the arithmetic performed on these numbers is increased; thus, double precision is used for mathematical operations requiring great reliability. Double-precision variables are declared using the words DOUBLE PRECISION. Because of the existence of double-precision variables, ordinary real variables are sometimes referred to as single-precision variables.

* * * * * * * *

Since FORTRAN was developed for use by mathematicians and engineers, you might guess that the language is exceptionally good at performing arithmetic and mathematical operations. You would be right. We won't go into all the mathematical possibilities of FORTRAN here, but we will touch on a few.

For instance, FORTRAN can be used to perform addition using the plus sign ("+"), as we saw above. A typical FORTRAN addition operation might look like this:

ISUM = NUMBER + 1760

Addition can be performed on all kinds of numbers: integer, real, double-precision, etc. We can also perform subtraction, with the minus sign ("−"), like this:

IDIFF = NUMBER − 4321

Multiplication is performed with an asterisk ("*"), like this:

IRESLT = NUMBER * 54

Double-precision variable—A variable that may be assigned a double-precision (generally, eight-byte) numeric value.

Division is performed with a slash ("/"), like this:

IQUOT = NUMBER / 3

Unlike the other arithmetic operations, division produces distinctly different results when performed with integer numbers than when performed with real numbers. Remember: An integer variable cannot contain a fractional value. The division operation, however, often produces fractional results. The fractional portion of the result will be lost if we attempt to store it in an integer variable. In some cases it does not matter whether the fractional portion is lost or not, but the programmer should give thought to this anyway.

In the above operation, for instance, we store the quotient of the operation NUMBER / 3 in the integer variable IQUOT. Suppose that NUMBER is equal to 10. The quotient, then, will be 3.3333... When we store this in the integer variable IQUOT, it will become, simply, 3. Of course, since this quotient contains an infinitely repeating decimal fraction, it would be difficult to store it accurately even in a real variable. Still, we would obtain much better accuracy in a real variable, where it might be stored as 3.3334, or some such. Computer arithmetic, you might note, is accurate only up to a certain number of decimal places. After that point, a variable may begin to store gibberish. We can increase the number of decimal places by using double-precision variables, but we cannot increase it indefinitely. For most purposes, however, computer arithmetic—and variable storage—is accurate enough.

We can even raise a number to a power by using double asterisks ("**"). Raising a number to a power refers to multiplying the number by itself a certain number of times. This is called *exponentiation*. For instance, to raise the number nine to the third power—that is, to multiply nine by itself three times—we would write:

9**3

Exponentiation—Raising a number to a power.

We can use more than one arithmetic operation in a single statement, like this:

RESULT = 4 * 6 + 2 − 1 / 5

You must be careful in programming such a sequence of operations, however. It is necessary to bear in mind the order in which the computer will perform these operations. If you have taken a course in algebra, you are probably aware that operations in such a statement are performed in a specific order. Exponentiations are performed first, in order from left to right, followed by multiplications and divisions, in the same order. Finally, additions and subtractions are performed.

This is also the order in which the computer will perform FORTRAN arithmetic. Consider the following set of operations:

5 + 7 * 3 / 4 − 8

Can you tell in what order the computer will perform these operations? First it will multiply 7 times 3, then divide the result by 4. Only then will it add 5 to the result of these operations and subtract 8 from the sum.

We can change this order, however, by using parentheses, another technique you may have encountered in algebra class. When the computer encounters an operation enclosed in parentheses, it will always perform that operation first. Of course, if it encounters more than one pair of parentheses, it will approach them in order from left to right. Consider the following:

(5 + 7) * 3 / (4 − 8)

In this example, the computer will add 5 and 7, then subtract 8 from 4, and only then perform the multiplication and division.

We can even place parentheses inside parentheses. In this case, the computer will work from the inside out. It will perform the operation in the innermost parentheses first, the next innermost parentheses second, and so on, until it works its way to the outermost parentheses.

* * * * * * * *

One thing you must be careful of in FORTRAN is *mixed-mode operations*. These are arithmetic operations that contain more than one type of number: both real and integer numbers, for instance. Some compilers allow mixed-mode operations, others don't. When compilers do allow mixed-mode arithmetic, the rule of thumb is generally this: The result of a mixed-mode operation will reflect the highest degree of precision in the operation. That is, the result of adding an integer and a real number will be real, but the result of adding a real number and a double-precision number will be double-precision.

Another tricky business is passing a value from a real variable to an integer variable. Consider the following series of assignment statements:

```
RLNUMB = 145.678
INUMB = RLNUMB
```

We will assume here that RLNUMB is a real variable while INUMB is an integer variable. RLNUMB is set equal to the real value 145.678. We then attempt to pass that value to the integer variable INUMB. However, INUMB cannot accept the fractional part of RLNUMB's value.

Some compilers will automatically remove the fractional part of the value. However, this is not always a good practice; the programmer may not recognize that this process has taken place, and an error might result. Fortunately, if we really need to pass a number from a real variable to an integer variable, FORTRAN offers us a special function with which this can be done. (A *function* is a series of oper-

---

Mixed-mode operation—An arithmetic expression containing variables and literal values of more than one type.

Function—A series of operations, generally identified by a single name, performed on a value or values and returning to a single value.

ations performed on a value, usually invoked with a single word.) This function is called INT. We use it as follows:

INUMB = INT(RLNUMB)

The INT function automatically removes the fractional value of RLNUMB and passes what is left to INUMB, so that INUMB is now equal to 145. Note that the value of variable RLNUMB is not affected by this operation, only the value passed to INUMB.

FORTRAN also features a number of other functions that can be used to perform elaborate mathematical operations, such as deriving the sine, cosine, log, or tangent of a number, finding the square root or absolute value of a number, etc. We won't be discussing these here; once again, if you wish to know more you should consult an advanced text.

* * * * * * * *

Here's a program that demonstrates some of the ways in which FORTRAN performs arithmetic:

```
C   A PROGRAM TO DEMONSTRATE FORTRAN
        ARITHMETIC
        INTEGER RESULT
        REAL NUMBER
        NUMBER = 1.453
        RESULT = INT(NUMBER /.007)
        ANSWER = RESULT * 4**2
        STOP
        END
```

This program declares the variable RESULT to be integer and the variable NUMBER to be real. Of course, we could have used these variables the other way around—RESULT as real and NUMBER as integer—and made the declarations unnecessary, but then we wouldn't have been able to demonstrate the use of the declaration statements.

NUMBER is assigned a real value, identified as such by the digits to the right of the decimal point. Division is then performed on variable NUMBER, and the result of that division passed to integer variable RESULT with the INT function. The value of RESULT is subsequently passed to the variable ANSWER, which is a real variable by virtue of its initial letter. This demonstrates that integer values can be passed to real variables without being explicitly altered.

We have now seen how to store and manipulate values in the computer's memory. But notice that though we have performed arithmetic in this program, we have no way of showing the user of the program that the arithmetic has been performed. If you compile and run this program with your FORTRAN system, the result will be a blank screen. You will have no way of knowing whether the program executed properly or not.

We need, then, to know how to get computed values back out of the computer's memory and into the hands of the computer user. This process is called output, and it is the subject of our next chapter.

Suggested Projects

1. Say which of the following names would be valid for FORTRAN variables:

OSTRICH
THIS
KNICK-KNACK
2001
1ST-ONE
HELP
NUM311
H!H!H!
HI!

2. Identify the following variable names as either integer or real.

ZORRO
APPLE
IGLOO
T12345
NIBBLE
WORK
JUMP

3. If a FORTRAN program begins with the line IMPLICIT REAL(K-Z), INTEGER (A-H), which of the variables in Project 2 would be integer, and which real? (Note that the IMPLICIT statement does not cover all possible variable names.)

4. Imagine that you sell pocket calculators. The calculators come in three varieties, which sell at three different prices: $9.95, $19.95, and $49.95. Last week you sold 212 of the first type, 106 of the second type, and 36 of the third type. Write a FORTRAN program that will calculate how much money you took in for all these sales. (Take note that the FORTRAN compiler will not understand the presence of dollar signs in a number.) Have the program store the total in a variable called TOTAL. Should this be an integer variable or a real variable? Will you need to write a declaration statement for it?

5. Suppose that the customers for your pocket-calculator business must pay a 5 percent sales tax on every calculator they buy. Write a FORTRAN program that will calculate how much sales tax was paid on the total arrived at in the last project.

4
GETTING INFORMATION OUT

In order to perform output in FORTRAN, you need a WRITE statement and a FORMAT statement. And that's all. You'll probably be amazed at the wide variety of output we can produce with those two instructions—such a wide variety, in fact, that we will only be able to scratch the surface in this book.

WRITE is an extremely versatile instruction. It can be used to send information to the video display, or to a disk drive, printer, tape recorder, or keypunch, should such devices be available. The FORMAT statement, in turn, specifies the form in which this information will be outputted. The syntax of a WRITE statement usually looks like this:

WRITE (output device number, FORMAT statement number) VARIABLE LIST.

The output device number is simply the number that has been assigned to the device to which you are sending output. This number has been assigned by your FORTRAN system. Check your manual to find out what the numbers are for your system. In this book we will use the numbers assigned by the Microsoft FORTRAN system used by the author. Be sure to change the numbers to conform to the system that you are using. The Microsoft device numbers are as follows:

Keyboard/video display	1, 3, 4, or 5
Printer	2
Disk drives	6, 7, 8, 9, or 10

Notice that some numbers have been assigned to both the keyboard and the video display. This should cause no confusion, since the keyboard is an input device and the video display is an output device, and thus one will be used only for input statements and the other only for output statements. Notice also that some devices have been assigned more than one number; you may choose the device number you wish to use. In this book, we will mostly be concerned with the video display and the keyboard, and we will use the number 5 to represent each.

The FORMAT statement number tells the compiler which FORMAT statement goes with which WRITE statement. You'll recall from the program we looked at in Chapter Three that FORMAT statement numbers appear in the column to the left of the FORMAT statements themselves. These numbers are chosen by the programmer while writing the program.

The VARIABLE LIST is optional. When used, it will cause the values of the variables in the list to be outputted to the chosen device.

A typical WRITE statement might look like this:

WRITE(5,11)

This tells the computer to send its output to device number 5, the video display, in the form specified by FORMAT statement number 11. Elsewhere in the program there should be a FORMAT statement that looks something like this:

11   FORMAT('0YOU''RE LOOKING GOOD!')

The FORTRAN compiler will allow you to place this FORMAT statement anywhere in the program that you wish, although it is generally a good idea to place it immediately after its associated WRITE statement; this will help make the program easier to read.

The result of placing these two statements in a FORTRAN program will be that the words YOU'RE LOOKING GOOD! will appear on the computer's video display. How does this work?

When the compiler encounters the WRITE statement, it immediately checks the relevant FORMAT statement to see what sort of output is required. In this case, it will see that we are merely asking it to output a string of characters—a message, that is. This string of characters must be inside single quote marks. These marks tell the compiler where the string begins and ends. If an apostrophe, which is identical to a single quote, is to appear within the quotes, it must be doubled, to tell the computer that it is not a quote mark.

The compiler will take a special look at the first character of that string, however, because this character tells the computer how many lines it is to space down on the video screen before producing output. If that character is a zero, as it is here, the computer will space down two lines. If the character is a blank space (" "), it will space down one line. If it is a plus sign ("+"), the computer will not space down at all but will begin writing information exactly where it quit after the last WRITE statement. Once it has performed the line spacing, it will write the rest of the string in almost all cases exactly as it appears between quotes.

You should be warned that the FORMAT statement above is not written strictly according to FORTRAN IV standards, although most compilers will be happy to accept it. However, if your compiler should reject it, the FORMAT statement can be rewritten like this: FORMAT(22H0YOU'RE LOOKING GOOD!). The letter H following the number 22 at the beginning of the string of characters tells the compiler that what follows is a *Hollerith literal*—a FORTRAN term meaning a string of characters. The number 22 in front of the H tells the compiler that the Hollerith literal will be twenty-two characters long, including the 0 character. This is a cumbersome way of writing strings of characters, but some compilers require it, and all compilers—including FORTRAN 77 compilers—will accept it.

Actually, very little of our output in a FORTRAN program is likely to be strings of characters, as in the above example; more often we will be outputting numbers, specifically, numbers that have been stored using variables. Fortunately, this kind of output can also be handled with a WRITE statement.

Hollerith literal—A FORTRAN term for a literal string of characters.

To output the value of one or more variables, those variables must be listed, one after another, immediately following the WRITE statement. For instance, if we wanted to output the value of the variables NUMBER and RESULT, we could use a WRITE statement something like this:

WRITE(5,66) NUMBER, RESULT

This statement outputs the values of variables NUMBER and RESULT to the video display in the manner specified by FORMAT statement 66. We could then pair this statement with a FORMAT statement that looks like this:

66   FORMAT(' ',I5,F7.2)

This FORMAT statement is chock-full of information, so let's analyze it piece by piece. The first character is a blank space between quotes; this tells the computer to space down one line before beginning its output. Following this, after a comma, we see an I5. This is a FORTRAN field descriptor (see p. 17). It tells the compiler the form in which the first variable is to be outputted. The I means that the value to be outputted will be an integer, and you'll notice that the first variable in the list following the WRITE statement is an integer variable, NUMBER. The 5 means that the computer is to allot five columns on the video display for writing the number represented by the variable.

Since most integer variables will contain five digits or less, this is probably adequate space. However, should the number turn out to be negative, we will need one space for the negative sign as well; thus, we might want to change this descriptor to I6, should there be a chance that the variable will contain a negative value. If the number is shorter than five digits, blank spaces will appear to the left of the number to fill out the nonexistent digits, like this:

..123

The periods in this example represent blank spaces within the field allotted for printing this value; they would not actually be visible on the computer's screen.

If the number is only three digits long, for instance, the computer will write two blank spaces to the left of the number to make up the difference. On the other hand, if the number is longer than five digits, you will get a field-width error while the program is being run. That is, a message will appear on the video display to tell you that the field descriptor did not allot proper width for the number that was to be outputted.

The second field descriptor reads F7.2. The F means that the second number to be outputted will be a real number. (You might wonder why FORTRAN uses an F rather than an R to represent real numbers. The F stands for floating point number, which is an alternate term sometimes used for real numbers.) The 7 tells the compiler that the number will be seven digits wide. The 2 following the decimal point tells the compiler that two of those seven digits will come to the right of the decimal point. If the number has more than two digits after the decimal point, they will be cut off and the last remaining digit rounded to the nearest fraction that will fit. If the number has too few digits to the right of the decimal point, the computer will supply zeros in the empty positions. If the number lacks sufficient digits to the left of the decimal point, the computer will supply blank spaces, as with integer numbers.

Incidentally, if we had added extra variables to the list in the WRITE statement—for instance, WRITE(5,66) NUMBER, RESULT, INUMB, TOTAL—the compiler would simply use the same FORMAT statement over and over again, as long as the FORMAT statement matches the variables that you use. For instance, after the second variable was printed, it would return to the beginning of the FORMAT statement and space down another line, then write the next variable using the I5 descriptor and the next variable using the F7.2 descriptor, and so forth.

Let's place the above statements into a larger program:

```
                NUMBER = 56
                RESULT = 345.7889
                WRITE(5,66)NUMBER, RESULT
66              FORMAT(' ',I5,F7.2)
```

The result of running this program is that the following will appear on the video display:

. . .56. .345.79

Notice the blank spaces, represented by periods here. There are three of them in front of the number 56—the three blank spaces required to fill out the five spaces allotted by the field descriptor. Then there are two more spaces in front of the next number—the two required to bulk out the seven allotted by that field descriptor. Notice also that only two digits follow the decimal point on the second number, although the original number contained four digits to the right of the decimal point; two have been trimmed off by the field descriptor. Observe that the computer has rounded the last digit up to the nearest value, rather than simply cutting it off after the second digit.

You might wonder why FORTRAN goes to so much trouble formatting its numerical output. Part of this goes back to the heritage of the keypunch machines. When punching information onto a punch card, it is essential that each hole be punched in precisely the right place. A hole punched one space too soon or one space too late might completely change the meaning of the computer's output. The area on a punch card assigned to a given unit of information is often referred to as a field; hence the term "field descriptor." This keypunch heritage will become even more apparent when we look at input field descriptors.

Another reason for the careful formatting is that FORTRAN is often used for producing printed reports containing many columns of figures. These columns must be formatted very carefully, with decimal points precisely aligned. This is especially true when producing reports containing columns of dollar values. The field descriptors allow us to carefully format information on a printed page.

Still, it would be nice if occasionally we could drop the field descriptors and simply write information as it is on the screen or on a page. FORTRAN 77 allows us to do this; alas, most versions of FORTRAN IV do not. It is possible to send unformatted information to the disk drive in FORTRAN IV; however, we will not be studying that technique in this book.

There are plenty of other things we could tell you about FORMAT statements and field descriptors, far more than we have room for here. We'll just try to tell you enough to get you writing FORTRAN programs of your own.

Often it becomes necessary to write blank spaces between values on the screen. This can be done by making the field width set by the descriptor wider than necessary, so that it will automatically place blank spaces between numbers, as we did in the last example given. We may also use the X descriptor. The X descriptor simply causes a blank space to be printed in the output. If we want to print more than one blank space, we can place the number of spaces in front of the X descriptor, like this: 4X. This will cause the computer to print four blank spaces at the point indicated.

We can add the X descriptor to our FORMAT statement above, like this:

66   FORMAT(1X,I5,5X,F7.2)

This will cause the computer to print five blank spaces between the first number and the second. Notice also that we've replaced the blank space between quotation marks at the beginning of the FORMAT statement with the X descriptor. This will still cause the computer to space down one line before writing the information; the X descriptor can be used interchangeably in this manner with the blank space inside quotes.

FORTRAN features a number of other field descriptors, though we will be discussing only a couple of them in this book. The I and F descriptors will probably suffice for most of our output. Perhaps the most interesting of the other descriptors, however, is the A descriptor. This descriptor causes *numeric information*—that is, numbers—to be outputted as *alphanumeric information*—that is, as characters and as strings of characters.

This may sound a little confusing. As a preliminary to explaining how to use the A descriptor, let's first comment

Numeric information—Information presented as numbers.

Alphanumeric information—Information presented as numbers and letters.

on the way in which computers store characters such as letters of the alphabet.

We said earlier that a computer's memory is able to contain only numbers. That's true, but often computers must deal with things other than numbers—words, for instance. Still, if we are to store such things in a computer's memory, we must convert them into numbers first.

There are several standard systems by which this conversion can be performed. The one generally used on microcomputers is called the *ASCII* (pronounced "askey") *code.* The name ASCII is short for American Standard Code for Information Interchange. The ASCII code assigns a number between 0 and 127 to every letter of the alphabet—a separate number for the uppercase and lowercase versions of each letter—as well as to the ten numerals (0 to 9) and to such common punctuation marks as the period and the semicolon.

When we use the A descriptor in FORTRAN, it tells the computer to interpret the numbers we are outputting as ASCII code numbers, assuming that your computer uses the ASCII code, as almost all microcomputers do. Consider this program:

```
C   A PROGRAM TO DEMONSTRATE THE 'A' DESCRIPTOR
          BYTE WORD1, WORD2, WORD3
          WORD1 = 67
          WORD2 = 65
          WORD3 = 84
          WRITE(5,39)WORD1, WORD2, WORD3
39        FORMAT(1X,3A1)
          STOP
          END
```

This program declares three byte variables—variables that take up only one byte of storage—and assigns them the values 67, 65, and 84, respectively. Then it writes these values to the video display using the descriptor 3A1. The number 3

ASCII code—A coding system used to represent alphanumeric characters.

in front of this descriptor is a *repeat factor*. It tells the compiler that this same descriptor is to be repeated with the next three variables. Such repeat factors can be used in front of any descriptors you wish, including the I and F descriptors. We've already used one with the X descriptor. The A tells the compiler that the information stored in the variables is to be interpreted as alphanumeric, and the 1 following the A tells the compiler that only one alphanumeric character is to be produced for each.

As a result of running this program, the following will appear on the video display:

CAT

Why did the computer write the word CAT on the video display? Because the numbers 67, 65, and 84 are the ASCII code numbers for the letters C, A, and T, respectively. Because the A descriptor tells the computer to interpret these numbers as ASCII codes, it prints the letters that the numbers represent rather than the numbers themselves. (With some compilers, we could have assigned values to the three byte variables like this: WORD1 = 'C', WORD2 = 'A', and WORD3 = 'T'.)

To summarize what we have learned about output, here is a program that will perform arithmetic on several numbers and print the results on the video display:

```
C         A PROGRAM TO DEMONSTRATE FORTRAN
          OUTPUT
          NUMBER = 14 * 17
          WRITE(5, 11)NUMBER
11        FORMAT(' FOURTEEN TIMES SEVENTEEN
          EQUALS ',I3)
          RESULT = 3432.12 / 666.678
          WRITE(5,21)RESULT
21        FORMAT('03432.12 DIVIDED BY 666.678
```

Repeat factor—A number in a field descriptor indicating that a descriptor is to be repeated the indicated number of times.

```
        EQUALS ',F8.4)
        STOP
        END
```

In this program, two arithmetic operations are performed, one of which produces an integer result (which is stored in an integer variable) and one of which produces a real result (which is stored in a real variable). The results of these operations are printed out separately, with an introductory comment. Note that the field descriptors in each FORMAT statement are specifically aimed at accommodating the output of their associated WRITE statements.

If you compile and run this program, you will see the following on your screen:

FOURTEEN TIMES SEVENTEEN EQUALS 238

3432.12 DIVIDED BY 666.678 EQUALS 5.1481

That's enough about output for now. Almost as important as our ability to get information out of a computer (or output) is our ability to get information into a computer (or input).

And that's the subject of the next chapter.

Suggested Projects

1. Write field descriptors for outputting the following numbers:

10
456.12333
−144
0.12
−111.111

2. Rewrite the sample arithmetic program from the last chapter so that it prints out the results of the arithmetic operations as they are performed.

3. Rewrite your programs for totaling calculator sales and computing interest (from the projects section of the last chapter) so that they print out the results with an appropriate sentence, such as THE TOTAL INCOME FROM CALCULATOR SALES LAST WEEK WAS, followed by the correct figure.

5

PUTTING INFORMATION IN

We get information into the computer the same way we get it out, except that for input we use a READ statement instead of a WRITE statement. The syntax for the READ statement is almost identical to that of the WRITE:

READ (input device number, FORMAT statement number)
    VARIABLE LIST

The input device numbers are the same as the output device numbers we saw in the last chapter.

In this book we will demonstrate programs that input information only from the keyboard. However, this is a little awkward in FORTRAN, because all the input field descriptors were originally designed to be used with punch cards, and thus the precise way in which the input is typed affects the way it is accepted by the computer, just as the precise way in which input appears on a punch card affects the way it is accepted by the computer. With keyboard input, a small typographical error can completely change the meaning of all subsequent input. Still, since most readers of this book will not have a card reader available, we will have to make do with keyboard input.

The field descriptors for input are the same as those for output, though they behave in a slightly different manner. In general, the descriptors divide each line of the computer's video display into a number of *fields*, just as on a punch

Field—An area in data storage or output allotted to a given data item.

card. Information typed within each of those fields is inputted to the computer and stored at the location of a specific variable.

Let's use an example. Consider the following READ statement and its related FORMAT statement:

                     READ(5,11)NUMBER, RLNUMB
11   FORMAT(I5,F7.2)

When these statements are encountered in a program, the computer will pause and wait for the user to type something on the keyboard. (Notice that we have specified input device number 5 in the READ statement.) Once that information is typed it will be stored at two locations in the computer's memory, those signified by the variables NUMBER and RLNUMB. Both are specified in the list of variables following the READ statement.

As this information is actually being typed into the computer by the user, it will, of course, appear on the video display. The FORMAT statement, however, divides the video display into a number of fields, which determines how this information must be arranged on the screen. (A field, you'll recall, was originally an area on a punch card used to hold a certain unit of information. In this case, the field becomes an area on the computer's video display used to hold a certain unit of information.)

What does this mean? Well, the first field descriptor is I5. This means that the first five spaces on the current line of the video display should be used to input an integer number. Anything typed after the fifth space on the screen will be ignored by this descriptor (though it will probably be picked up by the next one). If the number should end before the fifth space on the screen, the computer will add zeros to the end of it—which may not be what you had intended.

This is a tricky business. Let's suppose you type the following when the computer asks for input:

25678

Since this integer number appears in the first five positions on the screen, it will be inputted precisely as is. The number stored at the location NUMBER will be 25678. Note that we do not include commas in the number, so as not to confuse the computer. On the other hand, you might have typed:

−11245

Because the negative sign takes up one of the spaces in the five-character field, the last number falls off the end of the field and is ignored by the computer. Thus, the number inputted into the computer would actually be −1124, and the 5 would become part of the next field.

Suppose that you typed this:

.456.

This number begins in the second position of the field and ends one position short of the end of the field. The blank space at the beginning (here, a period) will be interpreted as a blank, which is probably what you intended, but the blank space at the end will be interpreted as a zero, which is quite possibly not what you intended. The number inputted into the computer would therefore be 4560. Given the field descriptor in the above FORMAT statement, the number 456 would be best typed as:

..456

Now there are two blanks in front of the number and none after.

The next field descriptor, F7.2, is somewhat more complicated in function. It tells the computer to expect a real number, using the F descriptor we encountered in the last chapter, typed into a field seven characters wide, which will immediately follow the five-character field created by the first descriptor. It also tells the computer that there will be a decimal point in this number and that there will be two digits after it.

This is the tricky part. It is not necessary that the decimal point actually be typed on the screen. If it is not there, the computer will assume it is there! For instance, suppose we typed the following:

.....1234567

Note that this number begins in the sixth position, which is the first position of the seven-character F field. The first five positions have been reserved by the first descriptor for the I field. This number will be inputted like this: 12345.67. Because we typed no decimal point in the input, the computer assumed it to fall between the fifth and sixth characters in the line, because the field descriptor indicates that only two digits will follow the decimal. Two-character decimal fields are very common when the values being inputted represent dollar amounts with decimal cents. On the other hand, suppose that we had typed a decimal point, like this:

.......12.4

This number begins in the eighth position rather than the sixth, so the computer assumes that all positions to the left of the 12 are blank spaces. Because we have actually typed a decimal point, the computer will honor our choice of positions for it. The number inputted, therefore, will be 12.40, which is probably what we had intended.

We can even use the X descriptor in a READ FORMAT statement. The X descriptor creates a blank field on the screen. Anything typed within this field is ignored. We may use this descriptor, therefore, to separate fields on the screen, like this:

FORMAT(I5,4X,F7.2)

This separates our I field from our F field by four spaces. Anything typed within these four spaces on the screen will be ignored by the computer.

As with WRITE statements, we may list as many variables as we like after a READ statement. If the computer runs out of field descriptors before it finishes the list of variables, it will return to the beginning of the descriptors and start again. We may also use a repeat factor with input descriptors, to indicate that they should be used with more than one consecutive variable.

We may even use the A descriptor with a READ statement. You'll recall from the last chapter that the A descriptor, when used in the output of values, causes the value of those variables to be interpreted as alphanumeric characters, according to the ASCII code. Similarly, the A descriptor can be used to input alphanumeric characters from the keyboard. The ASCII values of those characters will be stored in the indicated variables, like this:

```
11    BYTE CHAR1, CHAR2, CHAR3
      READ (5,11) CHAR1, CHAR2, CHAR3
      FORMAT (3A1)
```

This causes the computer to accept three characters from the keyboard and store their ASCII codes in the variables CHAR1, CHAR2, and CHAR3. If we typed the word CAT, for instance, the computer would store the ASCII codes for the letters C, A, and T in CHAR1, CHAR2, and CHAR3, respectively. We could print the word back out using the method shown in the last chapter.

Here is an example of a FORTRAN program that uses keyboard input. It accepts two numbers from the keyboard, performs mathematical operations on them, and writes the results on the screen:

```
C     A PROGRAM TO DEMONSTRATE FORTRAN INPUT
            STATEMENTS
            INTEGER     RESULT
            WRITE (5,11)
11          FORMAT('PLEASE   TYPE   TWO   INTE-
            GERS')
            READ(5,21)NUMB1, NUMB2
21          FORMAT(2I5)
            RESULT = NUMB1 + NUMB2
            WRITE(5,31)RESULT
31          FORMAT('THE  SUM  OF  THOSE  TWO
                  NUMBERS IS  ',I5)
            RESULT = NUMB1 - NUMB2
            WRITE(5,41)RESULT
41          FORMAT('THE DIFFERENCE IS   ',I6)
            RESULT = NUMB 1 * NUMB2
            WRITE(5,51)RESULT
51          FORMAT('THE PRODUCT IS   ',I10)
            RESULT = NUMB1 / NUMB2
            WRITE(5,61)RESULT
61          FORMAT('THE   INTEGER   QUOTIENT
                  IS  ',I5)
            STOP
            END
```

The action of this program is pretty simple. The trickiest part is typing the two integers that the computer will request when it executes the READ statement. The first integer must be typed in the first five positions of the screen while the second must be typed in the second five positions, because we are using an I6 descriptor with a repeat factor of two.

The program stores the two numbers that we type in the variables NUMB1 and NUMB2. It then performs a series of operations—addition, subtraction, multiplication, and division—on these numbers, storing the result each time in the variable RESULT, which we have declared as INTEGER for the occasion. It writes out each result immediately after we calculate it, along with an appropriate description. Notice that the value stored at RESULT is changed four times in the course of the program. We only need to retain each value long enough to write it on the screen.

The following program allows us to input temperatures in degrees Fahrenheit. It outputs those temperatures in degrees Celsius:

```
C    A PROGRAM TO CONVERT FROM FAHRENHEIT TO
     CELSIUS
     FORMAT (' + TYPE DEGREES FAHRENHEIT:   ')
     READ(5,11)FAHREN
11   FORMAT(1X,F5.1)
     CELSIU = (FAHREN − 32)* 5 / 9
     WRITE(5,21)FAHREN
21   FORMAT(F5.1,'   DEGREES FAHRENHEIT
        EQUAL   =')
     WRITE(5,31)CELSIU
31   FORMAT(F10.6,'+ CELSIUS')
     STOP
     END
```

The temperature in degrees Fahrenheit is contained in the variable FAHREN. The temperature in degrees Celsius is held in the variable CELSIU. After the conversion is performed, the results are printed on the screen. Each time you run the program you may enter a different temperature.

* * * * * * * *

Well, we've already accumulated quite an array of weapons in our FORTRAN arsenal. We have learned how to perform input and output, how to store information in memory, and how to perform arithmetic on that information. However, we have barely begun to scratch the surface of the wonders FORTRAN programming offers us. It is time now to take control of the very sequence in which a FORTRAN program is executed. Until now, we have allowed all instructions in our programs to execute one after the other, in the order they are written; in the next chapter we will learn how to change that, so that we can write programs far more complex and subtle than any we've attempted so far.

Suggested Projects

1. Rewrite your calculator sales program so that it accepts income information from the keyboard as the program is being run. Once rewritten, the program should be able to calculate new sales information every time it is run, depending on what information you choose to input.

2. Write a FORTRAN program that reverses our temperature conversion program so that it accepts temperatures in degrees Celsius and converts them to degrees Fahrenheit. Here is the formula for the conversion:

FAHRENHEIT = CELSIUS * 9 / 5 + 32

3. Write a program that accepts two numbers, raises the first number to the power of the second number, and prints the results on the display.

6

OUT OF ORDER

So far, we have shown only programs in which all instructions are executed in the order in which they are written,
from beginning to end. There will be many instances, however, when this will be undesirable. We will need to tell the
computer to execute instructions out of sequence. Most
commonly, we will need to tell the computer to execute a
sequence of instructions more than once. One of the
instructions that we use to cause the computer to execute
instructions out of sequence is GO TO.
　　Consider this:

```
10              WRITE(5,11)
11              FORMAT('  HELLO, THERE!')
                GO TO 10
                STOP
                END
```

Let's work our way through this program line by line. The
WRITE statement in the first line will write the words HEL-
LO, THERE! on the video display as specified by the
FORMAT statement on the second line; notice that the blank
space at the beginning of the FORMAT line tells the computer to space down one line before printing this. The next
line, however, tells the computer to GO TO (which means
exactly what it says) the line labeled 10. If we look in the
label column, we see that the first line is labeled 10; therefore, this instruction tells the computer to return to that
line and start executing instructions once again from that
point. Hence, the computer will write the words HELLO,
THERE! on the display a second time. Then it will reach the

GO TO instruction again, execute it, and return once more to the line labeled 10 and write the words HELLO, THERE! again, and so forth.

Note that the instruction STOP is never executed. The computer will continue looping through the first three lines of the program—forever, if we let it. The result is that we will see the following on the video display:

HELLO, THERE!
HELLO, THERE!
HELLO, THERE!
HELLO, THERE!
HELLO, THERE!
etc.

It is not considered particularly good practice to write a program that will not end. This is an especially dangerous practice when writing programs for large computers, where computing time is expensive and often in short supply. A program like this can eat up a lot of computer time for no good purpose; on a micro, it matters far less.

Still, if you've typed the program above, and compiled and run it, you might be wondering how you can get it to stop. The answer to this question will vary from system to system. On most, you will have to hit the computer's RESET button. Do this only as a last resort, however, because it will probably cause you to lose the program and any other information that you have in the computer's memory. Therefore, it is always good practice to save a FORTRAN program on a disk before running it, in case you have to hit RESET. Many FORTRAN systems save programs automatically before they are run, though you might check first to make sure.

A portion of a computer program that doubles back on itself, causing the computer to execute the same sequence of instructions more than once, is called a *loop*. If the loop never ends, in the manner of the loop above, it is called an *infinite loop*. (Some compilers will give a warning message if the program just compiled contains an infinite loop.)

Infinite loop—A program loop that will not stop executing as long as the program is running.

Loops are very important in programming, and most programs of any complexity will contain at least one. For instance, suppose we want to input a group of numbers in a program. We could do this by writing a series of READ statements. However, if the numbers are essentially identical in format, we could also input them like this:

```
10        READ(5,11)NUMBER
11        FORMAT(I5)
          GO TO 10
```

This program will read a series of numbers from the keyboard, one after another, and store each number in the variable NUMBER. After the computer reads a number, the GO TO statement will send it back to read the next one. Of course, nothing is done with these numbers after input, and each is lost when the next number is inputted, but this could be remedied with a little extra programming. We could, for instance, add each number to the sum of the previous numbers to create a running total, like this:

```
          ITOTAL = 0
10        READ(5,11)NUMBER
11        FORMAT(I5)
          ITOTAL = ITOTAL + NUMBER
          GO TO 10
```

The variable ITOTAL will now keep a running total of the values inputted into the variable NUMBER. When the loop ends, ITOTAL will represent the total of all numbers inputted while the loop was running. Notice that we set ITOTAL equal to 0 before we start the loop. This is called *initializing the variable,* that is, giving it an initial value. We do this because a variable in FORTRAN that has not actually been assigned a value will be holding whatever was in the computer's memory before the program was run. Always make sure that you initialize variables before using them as we used them above, or before writing their values to an output device.

Initializing a variable—Assigning an initial value to a variable.

There is a problem with this program. It represents another example of our new acquaintance, the infinite loop. It will never end. This loop cannot be of any use to us unless we have a way of terminating it.

One way of handling this is to give the computer some kind of decision-making capability, so that it can decide when it is time for the loop to end. This can be done by using a logical IF statement, like this:

```
        ITOTAL=0
10      READ(5,11)NUMBER
11      FORMAT(I5)
        IF (NUMBER .EQ. −1)GO TO 20
        ITOTAL = ITOTAL + NUMBER
        GO TO 10
20      WRITE(5,21)ITOTAL
21      FORMAT('THE TOTAL IS   ',I7)
        STOP
        END
```

Take a good look at the statement in the fourth line. This is a logical IF statement. It is extremely important. In fact, we'll print another copy of it right here:

IF (NUMBER .EQ. −1) GO TO 20

What does this line do? Pretty much what it sounds like it does. Translated into English, it says "If the value of variable NUMBER is equal to negative 1, go to the line labeled 20." The effect of this statement is to jump out of the loop as soon as we input −1. Therefore, inputting −1 becomes the way in which we tell the computer that the loop is over, which prevents the loop from becoming infinite. Once we have ended the loop, the program will proceed to print out the total of all the numbers we have inputted, with the exception of −1.

.EQ. means "is equal to." It is an example of what we call a *relational operator,* because it tests for a relationship

Relational operator—A symbol indicating, and testing, the relationship between two values.

between two values. The entire section of our logical IF statement that is enclosed in parentheses—the section following the word IF and preceding the GO TO—is called a *logical expression.* Like an arithmetic expression, a logical expression is a sequence of values and operations that has a single value, except that in the case of a logical expression that value is a logical value rather than a numerical one. There are only two logical values: true and false. Therefore, any logical expression has either the value "true" or the value "false."

The logical IF statement checks the value of the logical expression to see if it is true or false. If the logical expression is true, then the statement following the expression (in this case, GO TO 20) is executed. If the logical expression is false, then the statement following the expression is not executed.

There are a number of different relational operators that can be used to compare values in a logical expression. Here is a list of them:

.EQ.—is equal to
.GT.—is greater than
.LT.—is less than
.GE.—is greater than or equal to
.LE.—is less than or equal to
.NE.—is not equal to

We can create a wide range of logical expressions using these operators. For instance, if we want to terminate our program loop when *any* negative number is typed, we could change our logical IF statement to the following:

IF (NUMBER .LT. 0) GO TO 20

This causes the program to jump out of the loop if the number you input is simply less than (.LT.) zero. If we also wanted to jump out of the loop when the number zero was

---

Logical expression—A series of values and operators (including relational operators) that may be given a value of true or false.

inputted, we could change the logical IF statement to the following:

IF (NUMBER .LE. 0) GO TO 20

This causes the program to jump out of the loop if the number you input is less than or equal to (.LE.) zero.

Logical IF statements are extremely valuable. We need not use them only in conjunction with GO TO statements. We can also say things like:

IF (ANSWER .NE. QUESTN) RESULT = 12.555

In this example, we have told the computer that if the value of variable ANSWER is not equal to the value of variable QUESTN, then it should store the number 12.555 in variable RESULT.

This example, however, raises an important point. Unless we have previously told the computer otherwise, variables ANSWER and QUESTN are real variables, and performing comparisons on real variables is tricky at best. Remember that the value of a real variable is generally fractional, and that a fraction may have several decimal places. Therefore, it is unlikely that any two real variables will ever contain exactly the same number, which means that the expression REAL1 .EQ. REAL2 will almost never yield a true value. By the same token, our logical expression ANSWER .NE. QUESTN will almost always be true. FORTRAN programmers are advised to look for equality between real variables only at their own risk. A comparison such as REAL1 .LE. REAL2 or REAL 1 .GE. REAL2 is somewhat less dangerous and more likely to obtain a meaningful result.

We can pack more than one relational test into one logical expression by linking the tests together with *logical operators*. There are four logical operators in FORTRAN. They are .AND., .OR., .NOT., and .XOR.

Logical operator—A word that performs a logical operation—AND, OR, or NOT—on two or more logical expressions.

The first two of these operators mean pretty much the same thing in a FORTRAN program as they do when you use them in a sentence. Consider this logical IF statement:

IF ((VAR1 .LT. VAR2) .AND. (VAR3 .GT. VAR4)) GO TO 1000

This looks a little complicated at first, but if we wade through it step by step it begins to make sense. Translated into English, it would read "If the value of variable VAR1 is less than the value of variable VAR2 *and* the value of variable VAR3 is greater than the value of variable VAR4, then go to line 1000." The .AND. operator says, in effect, that both of these "relations" must be true before the entire logical expression is true—that is, before the GO TO statement can be executed. Notice, incidentally, that we have nested two sets of parentheses inside another set of parentheses, so that we will always know in what order these operations are to be performed; the .LT. and .GT. comparisons must be performed before the .AND. operation, or the whole statement ceases to make sense. Parentheses function in a logical expression exactly as they do in an arithmetic expression.

The .OR. operator functions in a similar manner. Consider this logical IF statement:

IF ((VAR1 .GE. VAR2) .OR. (VAR3 .NE. VAR4)) RESULT = 5 *
 X

Translated into English, this statement says "If variable VAR1 is greater than or equal to variable VAR2 *or* variable VAR3 is not equal to variable VAR4, then store the result of 5 times X at location RESULT." In other words, either of the two relational conditions must be true, or both of them may be true, if the assignment statement is to be performed. Only if neither of the two relations is true will the assignment statement definitely not be performed.

The .NOT. operator works a bit differently. It is usually placed in front of a relational statement; what it does is to reverse the value of that statement. If the relationship is true, then the .NOT. operator makes it false. If the relationship is false, then the .NOT. operator makes it true.

Confused? Here's an example:

```
IF (.NOT.(VAR1 .GT. VAR2)) GO TO 15
```

In this case, if VAR1 is greater than VAR2, then the statement .NOT. (VAR1 .GT. VAR2) is false; if VAR1 is not greater than VAR2, then .NOT. (VAR1 .GT. VAR2) is true—the precise opposite of what the result would be if we removed the .NOT. operator. Therefore, the GO TO statement will be executed only if VAR1 is less than or equal to VAR2. Translated into English, we could read this expression as "If VAR1 is *not* greater than VAR2, then go to line 15."

The .XOR. operator—sometimes called the "exclusive .OR." operator—works like the .OR. operator, except that the logical expression is true only if one or the other of the two statements linked by the .XOR. is true—*not* if both of them are true. For instance, consider this example:

```
IF ((VAR1 .EQ. VAR2) .XOR. (VAR 3 .LT. VAR4)) GO TO 1
```

This statement is true only if VAR1 equals VAR2 or if VAR3 is less than or equal to VAR4, but not if VAR1 equals VAR2 *and* VAR3 is less than or equal to VAR4. In short, it is true if one or the other of these two statements is true, but not if both are true.

Here is a program that uses a loop and several IF statements to create a guessing game where one player types a number on the computer keyboard and a second player tries to guess the number:

```
C   A GUESSING GAME FOR TWO PLAYERS
            INTEGER GUESS
10          WRITE (5,01)
01          FORMAT (' PLAYER 1: TYPE A NUMBER FROM 1
               TO 100 ')
            READ (5,11) NUMBER
11          FORMAT (I3)
            IF ((NUMBER .LT. 1) .OR. (NUMBER .GT. 100)) GO
               TO 10
20          WRITE (5,21)
21          FORMAT (' PLAYER 2: GUESS A NUMBER FROM
               1 TO 100')
```

```
30          READ (5,31) GUESS
31          FORMAT (I3)
            IF ((GUESS .LT. 1) .OR. (GUESS .GT. 100)) GO TO
               20
            IF (GUESS .EQ. NUMBER) GO TO 40
            IF (GUESS .LT. NUMBER) WRITE (5,41) GUESS
41          FORMAT (1X,I3,' IS TOO HIGH')
            WRITE (5,61)
61          FORMAT (' GUESS AGAIN ')
            GO TO 30
40          WRITE (5,71)
71          FORMAT (' YOU GOT IT!')
            STOP
            END
```

The rules of this game are simple. One player types a number while the other keeps his or her eyes averted. Then the second player tries to guess the number, typing each guess on the computer. The computer tells the second player if the guess is too high or too low. The game could be made more entertaining by keeping track of the number of guesses that each player makes, and comparing scores. You may be surprised how quickly you are able to guess a number within so large a range.

There are several GO TO loops within this program. Trace them on paper before running them on your computer, and see if you can predict how they will behave. Notice especially the lines where the computer checks to see if the player input is within the prescribed bounds: 1 to 100. A logical .OR. is used to make sure that the number inputted by the player is neither less than 1 nor greater than 100. If one of these conditions or the other is true, the program loops back to the WRITE statement that requested the input, giving the player a chance to correct the input error.

Once the number to be guessed has been inputted and stored in variable NUMBER, the computer asks for a guess from the second player, which is then stored in variable GUESS. This begins the main loop of the program. The computer will continue asking for numbers until the correct number has been guessed, at which point it will jump out of the loop and print the message YOU GOT IT! As long as the main loop continues executing, it will test the relationship between the number in NUMBER and the number in GUESS, and will tell the second player whether GUESS is higher or lower than NUMBER.

In creating program loops, it is often necessary to count the number of times that the loop has been executed. This can be done by establishing a variable that is equal to zero when the loop begins, then incrementing the value of the variable—that is, adding one to it—every time the loop is executed. When the loop is finished, this variable, which we call a *counter variable*, will contain the number of times that the loop has executed. This is especially useful when we want a loop to execute only a certain number of times, as we will see.

How do we increment a variable? Like this:

COUNT = COUNT + 1

This statement may look odd at first. Look at it closely and see if you can determine how it works. Essentially, it adds one to the current value stored in location COUNT and stores the new value back at location COUNT. In effect, it increases the value of COUNT by one.

Here is a loop that uses a counter variable:

```
        INTEGER COUNT
        COUNT = 0
10      COUNT = COUNT + 1
        WRITE (5,11) COUNT
11      FORMAT (I2)
        IF (COUNT .LT. 50) GO TO 10
        STOP
        END
```

What will this loop do if we run it? It will write the numbers from 1 to 50 on the video display of the computer, one after another; then it will stop. How does it do this? Each time the loop is executed, the value of COUNT is incremented by 1; then it is written to the display. When the value of

---

Counter variable—A variable used to count the number of times that a program loop is executed.

COUNT reaches 50, the IF statement in the sixth line will no longer loop the program back to the line labeled 10 and the loop will stop executing.

Counter variables have many different uses. However, there is another, more efficient way to create a loop like the one we just showed you, as we shall see in the next chapter.

Suggested Projects

1. Rewrite the guessing game program using a counter variable so that it counts the number of guesses made by the second player. Be careful where you place the counter variable within the loop. If improperly positioned, it may fail to count the final pass through the loop.

2. Write a program that will simulate a pocket calculator by accepting two numbers and an arithmetic operator, such as "+", "−", "*", and "/". Read the arithmetic operators into the byte variable OPER using the A descriptor, which will allow the user to input an alphanumeric character. Determine which operator was used with an IF statement like this: IF (OPER .EQ. 'A') GO TO 50. (Most FORTRAN IV compilers will accept this statement.)

3. Rewrite the temperature-conversion programs from the last chapter so that they will loop back endlessly for more input after each conversion is accomplished, thus saving the user from having to run the program each time he or she wants a conversion.

7

OUT OF ORDER
REVISITED

There is something you should know right now about computer programming. No matter how you choose to write a program, there will always be another way to write it, and often the other way will be better. But just as often, there will be yet another way that will be better still, and another. . . . For instance, FORTRAN offers us several other ways to write the loop programs that we studied in the last chapter, and some of these are better than the ways we used.

For example, there is the arithmetic IF. In some ways the arithmetic IF is like the logical IF. Both offer a way of letting the computer make a decision based on information available to it, but the arithmetic IF goes about this job somewhat differently.

Actually, it's quite a simple statement. It begins with the word IF, as in the logical IF statements we studied in the last chapter, and continues with an expression in parentheses. However, the expression must be arithmetic rather than logical. This expression, in turn, is followed by three numbers, representing line-number labels, separated by commas. Here is an example:

IF (NUM1 − NUM2)10, 20, 30

Like all arithmetic expressions, the expression in parentheses can be reduced to a single value, and that value must be negative, positive, or a zero. If the expression is negative, then the program will go to the program line bearing the label represented by the first entry in the list following the expression. If the expression is a zero. the program goes to the line with the second label in the list. If the expression is positive, the program goes to the third label. If that sounds more than a little confusing, the syntax of the arithmetic IF can be diagramed like this:

IF (arithmetic expression) neg. label, zero label, pos. label

Suppose that, in our program example above, the value of NUM1 is 4 and the value of NUM2 is −1. The result of the arithmetic IF statement is that the computer will immediately branch to line 30, because the value of 4 − (−1) is 5—a positive number. On the other hand, if the variables are equal to say, 8 and 11, then the program will branch to line 10, because the value of 8 − 11 is −3, which is negative. If both variables are equal to the same number, say 22, the program will branch to line 20, because the value of 22 − 22 is 0.

In the last chapter, we wrote a program that caused the computer to jump out of a loop if the value inputted into variable NUMBER was negative. Instead of using a logical IF combined with two GO TO statements—one to continue the loop and one to jump out of it—we could simply have used an arithmetic IF, like this:

```
          ITOTAL = 0
10        READ (5,11) NUMBER
11        FORMAT (I5)
          ITOTAL = ITOTAL + NUMBER
          IF (NUMBER) 20, 10, 10
20        WRITE (5,21) ITOTAL
etc.
```

The arithmetic IF statement checks the value of variable NUMBER (which constitutes an arithmetic expression all by itself, remember) to see if it is negative, a zero, or positive. If it is a zero or positive, the program branches back to line 10 and repeats the loop. If it is negative, however, it terminates the loop by leaping ahead to line 20. Thus, we have perpetuated the loop and offered a means of jumping out of it, all in a single program line.

There is one problem with this version of the program

that should be noted, however. The value of our terminating input—that is, the negative number that ends the loop—will be added into the value of TOTAL, just like all the other numbers that are inputted. This will cause the computer to print an inaccurate total; thus, the program would have to be changed somewhat before it could be used for any serious purpose. This should illustrate some of the problems that must be considered by the programmer in the creation of a loop. You must always notice where the loop begins and ends, and whether it accomplishes more or less than you wish it to.

There is yet another way to produce a loop in a FORTRAN program, and it is perhaps the best way of all. It requires only that we know in advance how many times we want the loop to repeat, but it also means that we will no longer have the liberty of terminating our loops with special input, as in the previous example. This is a small price to pay, however, for the advantages of using a DO loop.

The DO loop is FORTRAN IV's all-purpose looping structure. Most computer languages have at least one looping structure, and some have several. The way in which the DO loop works is rather complicated, so pay close attention.

A DO loop is established by use of the word DO. This word is followed by a number. The number corresponds to a statement number on a line elsewhere in the program; it tells the computer that the line with that particular label number is the last line in the loop. If the label on the last line of the loop is 40, for instance, we would write DO 40.

This, in turn, is followed by the name of an integer variable. By tradition, the variable used in DO loops is the variable I, although you need not find this tradition binding. This variable is called the *index* of the loop. The index variable is followed by an equals sign and two or three numbers separated by commas. These numbers are called the *initial value*, the *final value*, and the *increment value*, respectively. The increment value is optional. The index variable must

---

Index variable—The variable that is incremented throughout the execution of a DO loop.

be an integer variable; the other three values should be integers as well, and may be represented by integer variables, if you so desire.

Here is the syntax for a DO statement:

DO label index = initial value, final value, increment value

Before we tell you what each of these numbers means, let's watch them in action:

```
          DO 10 I=1, 15, 1
              WRITE (5,11) I
11            FORMAT (1X,I2)
10        CONTINUE
          STOP
          END
```

If you run this program, it will write the following on your video display. Note the similarity to the program in the last chapter that demonstrated the counter variable:

```
1
2
3
4
5
6
7
8
9
10
11
12
13
14
15
```

Why did it do that? Let's examine the DO statement:

DO 10 I=1, 15, 1

This tells us that the loop will extend from this line—the line on which the DO appears—down to the line labeled 10. The index of the loop is the variable I. Notice, incidentally, that we have indented all of the lines between these two points. This makes no difference to the compiler, but it does make it easier for a human reader to see which instructions are part of the loop.

The first time the loop is run, I is assigned the initial value of the loop, which is the number immediately following the equals sign. In this case, the initial value is 1; therefore I is assigned a value of 1. The next line writes the value of I to the video display, which is why the first thing the body of the loop does is to write a 1 on the display. Then line 10—the end of the loop—is encountered, and the computer automatically returns to the beginning of the loop, with the increment value added to the index. The increment value is the last of the three numbers following the equals sign. In this program, it is 1. When this is added to the value of the index, the index variable I becomes equal to 1 plus 1, or 2. The loop is executed again. The computer writes the current value of I to the video display—that is, it writes the number 2. When line 10 is encountered yet again, the computer goes back to the start of the loop. The value of the increment is added once again to the index, so that I is now equal to 3. This value is written to the video display, the loop repeats, and so forth.

The loop continues repeating until the computer ascertains that the current value of the index variable has exceeded the final value, which is the second number following the equals sign, or 15. After fifteen passes through the loop, I will equal 16. Because this exceeds the final value of the loop, the loop is automatically terminated. The computer then skips to the next line after line 10, which in this case contains a STOP command. The final value of I—16— is never printed to the screen, because the body of the loop is not executed again.

As we noted before, it is not always necessary to write the increment value of the DO loop. If the increment is 1, as in this case, we may also write the loop statement like this:

DO 10 I=1, 15

With no increment value stated, the compiler assumes an increment of 1. If you want an increment other than this, you must specify it. The following loop, for instance, will write every even number between 2 and 100:

```
                DO 10 I=2, 100, 2
                WRITE(5,11)I
11              FORMAT(1X,I3)
10              CONTINUE
                STOP
                END
```

What does the statement CONTINUE, which we placed at the end of the loop, do? Oddly, it does nothing; it simply gives the loop a place to end. There is a rule in FORTRAN that a loop must end on an executable statement. In the above program, we could not make the nonexecutable FORMAT statement the final line of the loop, although that would be necessary if not for the CONTINUE statement. Therefore, we end the loop on a CONTINUE statement, which is defined in FORTRAN as an executable statement even though it doesn't do anything. Also, the CONTINUE statement makes it visually obvious where the DO loop ends, which helps make the program easier to read.

The DO loop is extremely useful. To return to our earlier input loop, if we wanted to write it in such a way that we would be able to input five numbers, we could restate it with a DO loop, as follows:

```
                ITOTAL=0
                DO 50 I=1, 5
                READ(5,11)NUMBER
11              FORMAT(I5)
                ITOTAL = ITOTAL + NUMBER
50              CONTINUE
                WRITE(5,21)ITOTAL
21              FORMAT('  THE TOTAL IS   ',I6)
                STOP
                END
```

This loop reads five values from the keyboard, adds them together, and writes the result on the screen. Once understood, such a loop is simple to implement, and yet can be quite powerful if used correctly.

One instance in which DO loops can be quite powerful is when used in conjunction with arrays, which we will study in the next chapter.

Suggested Projects

1. In the following DO statement, identify which of the numbers and variables is the end-of-loop label, which the index, and which the initial value, the final value, and the increment:

DO 100 I = 7, VALUE, 5

2. Write a DO loop that will display every seventh number from 36 to 1,234.

3. Write a program that will add together the numbers from 1 to 10 and write the total on the video display.

8

ARRAYS

An *array* is a way of storing entire lists of information in a single, continuous area of memory, in such a way that you can call up any item in that list by a unique name that indicates its position within the list. The types of information that can be stored in arrays are the same as the types that can be stored in other variables; we may have integer arrays, real arrays, double-precision arrays, byte arrays, etc.

An integer array, to look at but one type, would be an entire series of locations in the computer's memory, one after another, each large enough to store a single integer. On a microcomputer, that means that each location would be two bytes long. We tell the computer how many such locations we wish to have in one array. It can be as few as two (or even one, though there would be no point in that) or as many as, well, as many as your computer's memory is capable of holding.

The nice thing about an array is that we can identify the entire array by a single variable name. Suppose, for instance, that we wish to establish an integer array in the computer's memory called IARRAY. We would do this with a DIMENSION statement, like this:

DIMENSION IARRAY(200)

Array—A sequence of variables containing a related sequence of values.

This tells the computer to make room in its memory for an array called IARRAY, containing two hundred separate elements, each of which requires its own separate memory location. The number of elements in the array is always placed in parentheses after the name of the array in a DIMENSION statement.

We can write the contents of array IARRAY like this:

```
           WRITE(5,11)IARRAY
11         FORMAT(1X,5I5)
```

This will write all two hundred items of array IARRAY on the video display of the computer, five to a line, as per the FORMAT statement. Of course, this might overflow the display a bit, but we could also use this method on a smaller array.

The main problem here is that what the computer will write on the screen is gibberish. We have yet to assign values to the elements of IARRAY; therefore, the locations within IARRAY might contain values left over from the previous contents of the computer's memory.

How do we assign values to the elements of IARRAY? There are several ways. On the whole, values are assigned to the elements of an array in much the same manner as they are assigned to individual variables: through assignment statements, or reading them from an input device, etc. However, when we make an assignment it is necessary to specify which element of the array we are assigning the value to.

This is done by placing the number of the element in parentheses after the name of the array. This number in parentheses is called the *array subscript*. Suppose, for instance, that we wish to assign a value of 29 to the fifth element of array IARRAY. We would do it like this:

```
IARRAY(5) = 29
```

Array subscript—A number in parentheses following an array name and indicating the position of an item within the array.

The number 5 in parentheses after the array name identifies the fifth element of array IARRAY, and the assignment statement sets that one element of the array (and no other) equal to 29. Similarly, we would assign a value of 469 to the 140th element of IARRAY like this:

IARRAY(140) = 469

The same method will serve for writing the value of individual array elements to the video display. We could write the 97th element of array IARRAY like this:

WRITE(5,11)IARRAY(97)

As we saw above, it is possible to write an entire array at one time to the video display by simply placing the name of the array in a WRITE statement. Suppose, however, that we only wish to write a certain range of elements from an array. We could use a DO loop. To write elements 44 through 77 of array IARRAY, we could use this loop:

```
         DO 10 I=44, 77
             WRITE(5,11)IARRAY(I)
11               FORMAT(1X,I5)
10           CONTINUE
```

Notice that we have expressed the chosen element of IARRAY as IARRAY(I). I is the index variable of the loop; therefore, it will assume all the values from 44 to 77 in the course of the loop. (The implied increment of the loop is 1.) Each time through the loop, the computer writes element I of IARRAY. The first time through the loop this is element IARRAY(44), because I is equal to 44; then element 45, when I is equal to 45; on through element 77, when I is equal to 77. Each value will be written to the display in its turn.

It is not necessary, however, for us to set up a complete DO loop to write all the elements of an array. FORTRAN allows us to use an implied DO loop in a WRITE statement. We could write the loop like this:

```
         WRITE(5,11) (IARRAY(I) I=44, 77)
11           FORMAT(I5)
```

This does exactly the same job as the loop before, but it is easier to write. The implied DO loop takes place entirely in the parentheses following the statement WRITE(5,11). It tells the computer to run variable I through all values between 44 and 77 (with an implied increment of 1), and to write the value of IARRAY(I) for each possible value of I.

If we wished to print out every third element of IARRAY from element 33 to element 99, we could write an implied DO loop like this:

WRITE(5,11) (IARRAY(I) I=33, 99, 3)

In this implied DO loop, the increment has been set at 3, so that the value of I jumps by amounts of 3: 3, 6, 9 . . . 96, 99.

It is sometimes awkward to assign initial values to the individual elements of an array. With an array of two hundred elements, like IARRAY, this could involve two hundred different assignment statements, which would not only be time-consuming to write but would take up an awful lot of room in your program and would slow down execution of the program terribly.

There is an alternate method for assigning values to the elements of an array, however. It is called the DATA statement. Suppose, for instance, that we have a five-element real array called VALUES. We could use a DATA statement to assign values to that array, like this:

DIMENSION VALUES(5)
DATA VALUES/1.56, 24.567, 456.1, 3.0, 4.5555/

The values assigned to the five elements of array VALUES appear between the slash marks after the name of the array. The first value is assigned to VALUES(1), the second value is assigned to VALUES(2), and so forth. We can also, incidentally, use a DATA statement to assign values to an ordinary, nonarray variable, like this:

DATA NUMBER/899/

or to a list of variables, like this:

DATA NUMBER, RESULT, ANSWER, VALUES/15.
4506.34,123.0, 5432.340, 11.11, 5.6, 7.0,−1234.56/

This **DATA** statement assigns values to the three variables NUMBER, RESULT, and ANSWER, and to the five elements of array VALUES, which we dimensioned earlier. The first value between slashes goes to NUMBER, the second to RESULT, the third to ANSWER, and the remaining five to the five elements of VALUES.

If we wish to initialize all elements of an array to the same value, our task becomes even easier. We can use the multiplication sign ("*") to create a repeat factor in an array statement, like this:

DATA IARRAY/200 * 0/

This fills all 200 elements of IARRAY with the value 0. Of course, we could use this with values other than zero, but zero is probably the value most commonly used for initializing arrays.

The chief advantage of assigning values with a **DATA** statement rather than an assignment statement is not that it saves you typing—though surely this is an important advantage—but that **DATA** is a nonexecutable FORTRAN statement and does not become part of the machine-language version of the program. It tells the compiler itself to store the values at the variable locations within the program so that the storage is accomplished while the program is being compiled, rather than while it is being executed. Assignment statements, on the other hand, become part of the machine code of the program. Therefore, assignment statements take up time, albeit a very small amount, while the program is executing; a **DATA** statement takes no time at all. Assignment statements take up space in the final program; **DATA** statements take up space only in the FORTRAN version of the program, not in the machine-language version. Therefore, you should get in the habit of using **DATA** statements rather than assignment statements wherever possible to initialize variables. However, remember that they may be used only to initialize a variable; an assignment statement is needed to change the value of a variable during the running of a program. For this reason, all **DATA** statements must go at the beginning of the program, before the first executable statement.

Another, rather obvious method of getting information into an array is through **READ** statements, while the program is running. This is a particularly good place for an implied DO loop. Our entire two-hundred-element array IARRAY could be initialized by a loop like this:

```
                READ(5,11) (IARRAY(I), I=1, 200)
11              FORMAT(I5)
```

Of course, this would be extremely tedious for the person inputting the values from the keyboard, but somebody has to do it, and it's quite possible that you won't even know at the time you write the program what values are going to go into it. In fact, the values inputted from the keyboard will quite possibly be different each time the program is run. If not, another loop could be used to store the values of the array elements on a disk or on punch cards, so that they could then be initialized from the appropriate mass-storage device the next time the program is run, saving everyone a great deal of work.

Now that we've explained how arrays can be set up within a program, perhaps we should turn to another question: What are arrays used for? The answer is, a great many things. Usually, we will store some kind of list of related items in an array. An array is particularly useful when we have a list of items that has to be kept in a certain order, or needs to be put in a certain order. For instance, we may use an array to hold a list of names and addresses. Alternately, we may use one array to hold the names and another identically dimensioned array to hold the addresses. We can input the names into the computer, via a READ statement, in any order that we like, then have the computer put them into another order—perhaps alphabetical according to last name. A program that puts an array into order like this is called a *sort program*. Sort programs are very common and very useful.

For example, here is a program that allows you to type integer numbers from the keyboard. These numbers are stored in the array VALUES. The program then sorts the numbers into numerical order and prints them in sequence

---

Sort program—A program that sorts an array into a meaningful order, such as alphabetic or numeric order.

on the screen. (Note that the numbers do not need to be—in fact, should not be—typed in numerical order.):

```
C    A PROGRAM TO SORT AN INTEGER ARRAY
          IMPLICIT INTEGER(A-Z)
          DIMENSION VALUES(10)
          WRITE(5,11)
11        FORMAT(' TYPE 10 NUMBERS.',' PRESS
     —        RETURN AFTER EACH:   ')
          READ(5,21) (VALUES(I), I=1, 10)
21        FORMAT(1X,I6)
10        FLAG=0
          DO 20 I=1, 9
              IF (VALUES(I) .LE. VALUES(I+1)) GO TO
                 20
              TEMP = VALUES(I)
              VALUES(I) = VALUES(I+1)
              VALUES(I+1) = TEMP
              FLAG = 1
20        CONTINUE
          IF (FLAG .NE. 0) GO TO 10
          WRITE(5,31)VALUES
31        FORMAT(1X,I6)
          STOP
          END
```

The particular kind of sort used here is known as a *bubble sort*. How does a bubble sort work? The computer works its way through an array of values—in this case, array VALUES—and compares each element of the array with the following element. If the first element is greater than the second, the computer swaps the two elements; otherwise, it leaves them as they were. Eventually, after enough such swaps have been performed, the elements of the array will be arranged in numerical order, though it may require several passes through the array before this is accomplished. How does the computer know when the array is in order?

Bubble sort—A kind of sort program where elements of an array are "swapped" in such a way that the array "bubbles" into the correct order.

When it is able to make a complete pass through the array without performing a single swap.

All of this is accomplished by the above program. The body of the sort is in the DO loop. Note that the initial value of the loop is the same as the subscript of the lowest element of the array and that the final value of the loop is the same as the subscript of the second highest element of the array. (This makes sense, as the final element of the array has no next higher element to be compared with.) The computer then compares each element with its succeeding element and performs a swap if necessary. Note that a third variable, TEMP, is required for temporary storage of one of the values while the swap is being performed. If you think about it for a moment, the reason for this should be obvious.

Notice also that a variable called FLAG is set equal to zero before the loop is executed. When a swap is performed, FLAG is set equal to 1. At the end of the loop, the computer checks to see if FLAG has remained equal to zero. If it has—which would indicate that no swaps were performed—the computer writes out the sorted array. Otherwise, it jumps back and executes the loop again.

Compile and run this program. Type in ten numbers as requested and press RETURN after each. You'll be surprised by how quickly the computer performs the sort— almost before your finger is off the RETURN key.

Another use for arrays is the storage of words and sentences. Earlier, we saw that the A descriptor could be used to prepare the computer for alphabetic input and output. If the A descriptor is used, we can persuade the computer to fill a byte array with characters typed from the keyboard, and to print those characters out as a single string.

This program will accept the user's name from the keyboard and will respond in kind:

```
11        BYTE STRING(20)
          WRITE(5,11)
21        FORMAT(' WHAT IS YOUR NAME?  ')
          READ(5,21) (STRING(I), I=1, 20)
31        FORMAT(20A1)
          WRITE(5,31)STRING
          FORMAT(' NICE TO MEET YOU,  ',20A1)
          STOP
          END
```

Notice that we have dimensioned array STRING without benefit of a DIMENSION statement. The dimensioning was done in the BYTE statement, which not only declares STRING(20) to be a byte variable but to be a byte variable array with twenty elements. This is perfectly acceptable to the FORTRAN compiler and can also be used with other types of arrays, such as integer and double-precision.

Once the array has been dimensioned, the computer will proceed to fill the array with the ASCII code numbers of the characters that you type on the keyboard, as per the A descriptor. (See Chapter Five.) If you run the program, you will notice that it is not necessary, despite the implied DO loop in the READ statement, to type all twenty elements into the array. Rather, pressing RETURN will terminate the READ statement.

The computer will then write the contents of the array as a series of ASCII characters. If you followed the instructions in the program and typed your name, the result might look like this:

WHAT IS YOUR NAME? JOE DOAKS

NICE TO MEET YOU, JOE DOAKS

The first JOE DOAKS is the one that *you* typed (unless, of course, your name is not Joe Doaks). The second is the one that the *computer* typed when it printed out the contents of array STRING.

We can even create arrays with more than one dimension. This may be a little hard to grasp, but essentially a *multi-dimensional array* is an array where the elements are identified by more than one subscript, like this:

IARRAY(15, 23)

We dimension a multi-dimensional array like this:

DIMENSION IARRAY(100, 200)

Multidimensional array—An array where each item has more than one subscript, indicating a complex network of relationships between items.

Note that although we have used an array here with the same name as a differently dimensioned array earlier in this chapter, you are not allowed to do this within a single program. A single array name may not appear in more than one DIMENSION statement.

This DIMENSION statement establishes a 100- by 200-element, two-dimensional array—that is, an array with two subscripts—in the computer's memory called IARRAY. How many elements are there in array IARRAY now? A phenomenal 20,000 elements (100 multiplied by 200). If IARRAY is an integer array, it will take up 40,000 bytes of memory in a microcomputer—more than many computers will even have available for variable storage. We mention this only to point out that multi-dimensional arrays can eat up a lot of space, and you should be careful how many elements you use in each dimension. You might find yourself unexpectedly short of room.

Why would we create a two-dimensional, 100- by 200-element array instead of a one-dimensional 20,000-element array? For reasons of organization, mostly. In certain instances, it is easier to keep the elements of an array logically organized in two dimensions than in one. Consider, for instance, if we wanted to create a chessboard.

A chessboard can be thought of as a two-dimensional array with eight elements in each dimension, for a total of sixty-four elements (each representing one of the board's sixty-four squares, which are arranged eight to a side). We would dimension such an array like this:

DIMENSION BOARD(8, 8)

This creates a two-dimensional, eight-by-eight, real array called BOARD, with each element of the array being equivalent to a square on the chessboard. To set up a chess game, we would set each element of the array equal to whatever playing piece happened to be sitting on it at the moment. We could initialize this array like this:

```
      DATA BOARD/'B-RK','B-KN','B-BI','B-QN','B-KI',
    - 	'B-BI','B-KN','B-RK',8*'B-PN',32*
    - 	'  --  ',8*'W-PN','W-RK','W-KN','W-BI',
    - 	'W-QN','W-KI','W-BI','W-KN','W-RK'/
```

We have done something very odd in this DATA statement, something that deserves further explanation. We have initialized the elements of a real array as words, rather than as numbers.

Remember when it was pointed out earlier that a real number takes up four bytes of memory storage? And remember when we showed how the contents of a byte variable could be written (or initialized) as characters rather than as numbers? Well, FORTRAN allows us to write or initialize real variables as four characters apiece, because each real variable is the equivalent of four byte variables. When we set an element of real array BOARD equal, say, to 'B-RK' (which stands, on our chessboard, for "black rook"), we are actually setting it equal to the ASCII code numbers for the four characters "B," ""-, "R," and "K." We then must write it back out using the A descriptor, which will interpret these code numbers as letters.

In our DATA statement, the elements of array BOARD are initialized in this order:

BOARD(1,1), BOARD(2,1), BOARD(3,1) . . . BOARD(7,8),
    BOARD(8,8)

Notice that the first subscript changes faster than the second. This means that in our DATA statement we have assigned the value 'B-RK' ("black rook") to BOARD(1,1), the value 'B-KN' ("black knight") to BOARD(2,1), and so forth.

The other chess pieces represented here are the 'B-BI' ("black bishop"), 'B-QN' ("black queen"), 'B-KI' ("black king"), 'B-PN' ("black pawn"), and so forth. Each of these pieces has its white ('W') equivalent at the opposite end of the array, which is to say the opposite side of the board. Elements set equal to ' -- ' represent unoccupied squares on the chessboard.

Okay, so we've set an array equal to all the pieces on a chessboard. What good does this do us? Well, the next thing we need is a method of printing out this array in such a way as to form a visible chessboard on the computer's screen. Perhaps this routine will suffice:

```
DIMENSION BOARD(8,8)
DATA BOARD/'B-RK', 'B-KN', 'B-BI', 'B-QN',
```

```
                    'B-KI', 'B-BI', 'B-KN', 'B-RK',8*'B-PN',32*
               '  --  ',8*'W-PN', 'W-RK', 'W-KN', 'W-BI',
               'W-QN', 'W-KI', 'W-BI', 'W-KN', 'W-RK'/
               WRITE(5,11)BOARD
11             FORMAT(1X,8A5)
               STOP
               END
```

Notice how simple it is to print out the chessboard once we have properly arranged it within the array. The WRITE statement following the DATA statement does the actual writing; since we specify the array BOARD without a specific subscript, it simply writes out the entire array. The FORMAT statement on line 11 tells it how to write the array: with a carriage return, followed by eight elements of the array (as per the repeat factor of 8), then another carriage return (because the FORMAT statement will be repeated until all elements of the array are written), followed by another eight elements, and so on. Notice that we have set a field width of 5 for writing each element of the array, despite the fact that we know each element to require only four spaces on the display. This automatically leaves a space between each element on the screen, for readability.

When the array is written out, it will look like this:

B-RK	B-KN	B-BI	B-QN	B-KI	B-BI	B-KN	B-RK
B-PN	B-PN	B-PN	B-PN	B-PN	B-PN	B-PN	B-PN
--	--	--	--	--	--	--	--
--	--	--	--	--	--	--	--
--	--	--	--	--	--	--	--
--	--	--	--	--	--	--	--
W-PN	W-PN	W-PN	W-PN	W-PN	W-PN	W-PN	W-PN
W-RK	W-KN	W-BI	W-QN	W-KI	W-BI	W-KN	W-RK

And there you have it. A complete chessboard, set up and ready to play.

Moving pieces on the board would simply be a matter of swapping values from one array element to another. An experienced programmer could take this simple beginning and write a program that would actually be capable of playing chess against a human player, though this would be a rather formidable problem in programming.

This, of course, is too complex a project for a beginning programmer, and we are not suggesting that you attempt it. However, if you are feeling especially ambitious, you might try instead to write a program for some simpler game, such as checkers, tic-tac-toe, or even a card game. In a card game, the deck of fifty-two cards could be represented by a fifty-two-element array called, say, DECK. Each player's hand could also be represented by an array of appropriate size—seven elements in a game of seven-card stud, for instance, or five in a game of five-card draw.

Before you attempt any of these projects, however, you might want to tackle a more advanced book on the subject of FORTRAN programming, or on programming techniques in general. Still, it couldn't hurt to consider the ways in which you would attempt such a project.

Suggested Projects

1. Write a program that finds the largest number in an array. Such a program would accept a series of numbers from the keyboard, store them in an array, then search through the list to find the largest value, which it would print on the display. Rewrite the program so that it finds the smallest value in the array.

2. Write a program that accepts a series of alphanumeric characters from the keyboard, then sorts those characters into alphabetic order. (This can be done by comparing the byte variables used to hold the characters and placing them in numeric order according to the values held in those variables.) Use a bubble sort such as the one used in this chapter.

9

SUBPROGRAMS

There is one other way in which FORTRAN makes life easier for programmers. It is called the *subprogram*. The FORTRAN subprogram is a complete little, and sometimes not-so-little, program that can be attached to the end of a regular FORTRAN program. It has its own separate set of variables, unrelated to those in the main program. And even if a variable in the subprogram has the same name as a variable in the main program, it will not be affected by the value of the variable in the main program. It is possible to pass information back and forth between the main FORTRAN program and the subprogram, but only in carefully defined ways.

What good is a subprogram? Well, each subprogram generally performs a single task, or a closely related set of tasks. Suppose that in the course of your main program you wish to perform a task that you have already performed in an earlier program, and you don't want to go to the trouble of writing the instructions for it again. Or suppose you need to perform the same task at several different places in your main program and don't want to rewrite, or retype, the instructions each time. You can "call" a subprogram to do the task for you. An example of such a task might be sorting an array, or finding the average of several numbers.

Subprogram—A separate program at the end of a FORTRAN program; the subprogram has its own variables and may be "called" by the main program to perform a task and return a value (s).

One common kind of subprogram is the *subroutine*. Subroutines are called via the CALL instruction. To take a hypothetical example, imagine that in writing a program you discover that it is necessary to clear all writing from the display for a moment so that you can begin writing on the display once again with a clear slate, as it were. Perhaps we could write a subroutine to perform this task, and give the subroutine the name CLEAR. It is difficult to describe how such a subroutine might work, since the best possible implementation would vary from computer to computer. The following, however, is a rather makeshift way in which it could be done:

```
          SUBROUTINE CLEAR
          DO 10 I=1,1920
            WRITE(5,11)
11            FORMAT('+   ')
10          CONTINUE
          RETURN
          END
```

This routine writes 1,920 blank spaces on the display, one after another. This assumes, of course, that your video display has 24 lines of 80 characters apiece, for a grand total of 1,920 spaces. Actually, there are less awkward, and possibly more effective, ways of performing this task, but they will vary from computer to computer, and we are simply using this as an example.

The first line of the subprogram identifies it as a subroutine named CLEAR. The statement RETURN at the end of the program indicates that the computer may return to executing the instructions in the main program once again. You may place more than one RETURN statement in a subroutine if you like. This gives the computer the alternative of exiting the subroutine at several different points. (Perhaps an IF statement could decide which exit is to be taken at any given time.) At the end of the subroutine, the word

---

Subroutine—A kind of subprogram called via a CALL instruction.

END must appear, so that the compiler knows when the subroutine is complete.

To use this subroutine in the main FORTRAN program, we invoke it with the words CALL CLEAR. Here is an example of a FORTRAN program using this particular subroutine:

```
C   PROGRAM TO DEMONSTRATE THE USE OF
        SUBROUTINES.
            CALL CLEAR
            READ(5,11)I,J
11          FORMAT(2I5)
            CALL CLEAR
            K = I + J
            WRITE(5,21)K
21          FORMAT(I5)
            STOP
            END
C   END OF MAIN PROGRAM, BEGINNING OF
        SUBROUTINES
            SUBROUTINE CLEAR
            DO 10 I=1,1920
                WRITE(5,11)
11              FORMAT('+')
10          CONTINUE
            RETURN
            END
```

The main program calls the subroutine CLEAR twice, once before it reads input and once before it displays the sum of the two numbers that were read from the keyboard. Notice that we still end the main body of the program with the word END, and only then begin the subroutine, which in turn also ends with the word END. Thus, the compiler knows where the main program ends and the subroutine begins. In this fashion, we can chain as many subroutines, one after another, as we wish, with each new subroutine beginning after the word END that terminated the last one.

Sometimes it is necessary to pass the value of variables from the main program to a subroutine. This is usually done with a *parameter list*. There are other ways, but we won't be discussing them in this book. The parameter list is a list of values that appears in the subroutine call, corresponding to a list of variables that follows the subroutine name. To demonstrate, let's concoct a program that uses a subroutine for the simple task of adding two numbers together:

```
        READ(5,11)NUMB1, NUMB2
11      FORMAT(2I5)
        CALL ADD(NUMB1, NUMB2, NUMB3)
        WRITE(5,21)NUMB3
21      FORMAT('  THE TOTAL IS',I5)
        STOP
        END
        SUBROUTINE ADD(IVAL1, IVAL2, IVAL3)
        IVAL3 = IVAL1 + IVAL2
        RETURN
        END
```

Subroutine ADD doesn't do much that we couldn't have done in the main program, but, once again, it illustrates our point. Notice following the subroutine call that the names of three variables from the main program (NUMB1, NUMB2, NUMB3) appear in parentheses. This is called the parameter list. Notice also that there is a similar list of parameters following the name of the subroutine at the beginning of the subroutine listing itself. The parameters in that list have different names than the parameters in the main program, but there are also three of them: IVAL1, IVAL2, and IVAL3.

When we call the subroutine, the values stored in the locations represented by the variables in the parameter list are automatically passed to the subroutine. They are matched with the parameters in the list following the subroutine name in the subroutine itself. In other words, the parameters IVAL1, IVAL2, and IVAL3 are automatically set equal to the values of the parameters NUMB1, NUMB2, and

Parameter list—The list of values, in parentheses after the subprogram call and subprogram name, that are passed back and forth between the subprogram and the main program.

NUMB3. Note that this passing of values takes place according to the order of the values in the list. The value of the first parameter in the parameter list is passed to the first parameter in the subroutine; the second value is passed to the second parameter; and so on. It is up to the programmer to make sure that all of these parameters are in place in their respective lists, and that the number of parameters in each list corresponds to the numbers in the other list. That is, if three parameters follow the subroutine call, then three parameters should follow the subroutine name.

This passing of values takes place both ways. When subroutine ADD is complete, the current values of IVAL1, IVAL2, and IVAL3 are passed back to the variables NUMB1, NUMB2, and NUMB3 in the main program. This is why our main program proceeds to treat the variable NUMB3 as though it contains the total of NUMB1 and NUMB2. It does, because subroutine ADD performed the addition and passed the sum back to NUMB3.

Here is our sort program from the last chapter, rewritten using subroutines:

```
C     A PROGRAM TO SORT AN INTEGER ARRAY
            IMPLICIT INTEGER(A-Z)
            DIMENSION VALUES(10)
            WRITE(5,11)
11          FORMAT('TYPE 10 NUMBERS.',' PRESS
      -     RETURN AFTER EACH:   ')
            READ(5,21) (VALUES(I), I=1, 10)
21          FORMAT(1X,I6)
            CALL SORT(VALUES)
            WRITE(5,31)VALUES
31          FORMAT(1X,I6)
            STOP
            END
            SUBROUTINE SORT(ARRAY)
            IMPLICIT INTEGER(A-Z)
10          FLAG=0
            DO 20 I=1, 9
            IF (ARRAY(I) .LE. ARRAY(I+1)) GO TO 20
            TEMP = ARRAY(I)
            ARRAY(I) = ARRAY(I+1)
            FLAG = 1
20          CONTINUE
            IF (FLAG .NE. 0) GO TO 10
            RETURN
            END
```

The only difference between this and the earlier version of the program is that now we call SORT as a subroutine, rather than simply leaving the sort routine in the main program. The chief advantage of this is that we can save subroutine SORT on our disk as though it were a separate program, then add it to the end of any program in which we need an integer sort. The problem with this is that subroutine SORT can work only with an array of ten elements. We might wish to use it with an array containing more, or fewer, elements. We could rewrite it for every use, of course, but we would be better off if we used a parameter for the size of the array, and passed the value to it from the main program. The DO loop in the sort would look like this:

DO I=1, FINAL

The subroutine would be declared like this:

SUBROUTINE SORT(ARRAY, FINAL)

And it would be called like this:

CALL SORT(ARRAY, FINAL)

There is another type of FORTRAN subprogram as well: the FUNCTION. This is similar to the functions that we discussed in an earlier chapter; however, instead of forcing the programmer to use functions that are already built into the FORTRAN compiler, the FUNCTION subprogram allows the programmer to invent his or her own functions and call them up with a single word.

Suggested Projects

1. Look through the program examples that we have used in earlier chapters, and the programs that you have written as projects. Decide which ones could be rewritten with the use of subroutines and rewrite them. Does the use of subroutines make the programs easier to understand? Does it make them shorter? Easier to write?

2. Choose a programming project of your own devising. You now know enough about the FORTRAN language to develop a fairly ambitious one. Decide on what you want to write, make notes on paper as to how it should be written, and write the program. Run it. Rewrite it if it doesn't work. Pat yourself on the back when it does.

10

WELCOME TO THE REVOLUTION!

In summary, it would seem fair to say that the FORTRAN language offers a wide array (no pun intended) of useful techniques for both the fledgling and the expert computer programmer. It is a mature language, in the sense that it has been around as long as or longer than any other high-level language, and it has evolved with the times, changing as the needs of programmers have changed. Perhaps someday you will also be interested in exploring FORTRAN 77, the current standard version of this programming language. FORTRAN 77 offers all of the features included in FORTRAN IV, some of which we have not even had time to cover in this book, plus others; this gives programmers the option of utilizing whichever programming technique seems best for a given situation.

Whether you choose to go on to study more advanced programming, or simply use this book to open your eyes—and your mind—to the possibilities of the computer age, you have probably profited from the experience. Almost certainly there is a computer in your future; perhaps there is already one in your present, or more than one. And you now can approach it with a degree of understanding, rather than the confusion and apprehension that so many people have brought to the computer revolution.

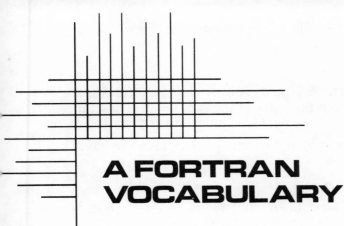

A FORTRAN VOCABULARY

RESERVED WORDS

BYTE. Declares a variable as a byte variable.

CALL. Calls a FORTRAN subroutine.

CONTINUE. An executable statement that does nothing; generally used as the termination of a DO loop.

DATA. Initializes the variables in a variable list to the values in a value list.

DIMENSION. Establishes a variable array of a specific number of elements.

DO. Introduces a loop; must be followed by the terminal label of the loop, the index variable, the starting value, the ending value, and, optionally, the increment value.

DOUBLE PRECISION. Declares a variable as a double-precision variable.

END. Tells the compiler that the program is complete.

FORMAT. Precedes a list of field descriptors giving the format for output or input of variable data in the related WRITE or READ statement.

GO TO. Transfers program control to the line with the label given after the words GO TO.

IF (arithmetic). Evaluates an arithmetic expression and transfers program control to one of three listed addresses, depending on whether the value of the expression is negative, zero, or positive.

IF (logical). Evaluates a logical expression and executes the following statement if the value of the expression is false; if not, control passes to the next statement in the program.

IMPLICIT. Declares an alphabetic range of variables to have a stated default type.

INTEGER. Declares a variable as an integer variable.

READ. Inputs a value from an input device and stores it in a variable, according to the related FORMAT statement.

REAL. Declares a variable as a REAL variable.

RETURN. Returns control from a subroutine to the statement following the subroutine call.

STOP. Halts execution of a program.

SUBROUTINE. Declares a subprogram, with the name following the word SUBROUTINE.

ARITHMETIC OPERATORS

+ addition
− subtraction
* multiplication
/ division
** exponentiation

RELATIONAL OPERATORS

.GT. greater than
.LT. less than
.EQ. equal to
.GE. greater than or equal to
.LE. less than or equal to
.NE. not equal to

LOGICAL OPERATORS

.AND.
.OR.
.NOT.
.XOR.

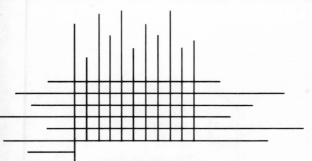

INDEX